Southern Writers

PRENTICE HALL
Upper Saddle River, New Jersey
Needham, Massachusetts

ISBN 0-13-435448-6

7 8 9 10   02 01

PRENTICE HALL

Acknowledgments

Grateful acknowledgment is made to the following for copyrighted material:

Margaret Walker Alexander

"Childhood" from *This Is My Century* by Margaret Walker, published by University of Georgia Press. Copyright © 1989. Reprinted by permission of the author.

Doubleday, a division of Bantam Doubleday Dell Publishing Group, Inc.

"The Rain Guitar" from *The Strength of Fields* by James Dickey. Copyright © 1979 by James Dickey. Used by permission of Doubleday, a division of Bantam Doubleday Dell Publishing Group, Inc.

The Heirs of the Estate of Martin Luther King, Jr., c/o Writers House, Inc. as agent for the proprietor

"I've Been to the Mountaintop" by Martin Luther King, Jr. Copyright © 1968 by Martin Luther King, Jr., copyright renewed 1996 by The Estate of Martin Luther King, Jr. Reprinted by arrangement with The Heirs of the Estate of Martin Luther King, Jr., c/o Writers House, Inc. as agent for the proprietor.

Farrar, Straus, & Giroux, Inc.

"Enoch and the Gorilla" and "The Crop" from *The Complete Stories* by Flannery O'Connor. Copyright © 1971 by the Estate of Mary Flannery O'Connor. Reprinted by permission of Farrar, Straus, & Giroux, Inc.

Harcourt Brace & Company

"Eagle Rock" by Alice Walker from *Revolutionary Petunias & Other Poems*, copyright © 1971 by Alice Walker. "A Visit of Charity" by Eudora Welty, from *A Curtain of Green and Other Stories*, copyright 1941 and renewed 1969 by Eudora Welty.

Houghton Mifflin Company

"Wonderkind" from *The Ballad of the Sad Café and Collected Short Stories* by Carson McCullers. Copyright © 1936, 1941, 1942, 1950, © 1955 by Carson McCullers. Copyright © renewed 1979 by Floria V. Lasky. Reprinted by permission of Houghton Mifflin Company. All rights reserved.

(Acknowledgments continue on p. 146.)

Contents

Introduction

Certain writers can make a place come alive through their writing. This is especially true of those who come from the Southern United States. In the voices of these writers you can feel the heat of the Georgian sun, see the beauty of the Appalachian Mountains, and hear the call of the mockingbird. You can also experience the devastation of the Civil War and the struggles of generations of people who have fought for tolerance and freedom from oppression.

In this anthology you will hear the voices of nineteen writers from eight Southern states—from the opening selection, an impassioned testament to democracy by Thomas Jefferson, to the final essay, a reflective essay on cats by North Carolina writer John Holman. On the pages in between you'll encounter two hundred years of writing steeped in the strong literary traditions of the South.

From the nineteenth century come the works of two poets whose lives and writing were strongly influenced by the catastrophic events of the Civil War. These are followed by a moving personal account of Booker T. Washington's fierce desire to attend a school for young African Americans.

The anthology moves into the twentieth century with a poem by John Crowe Ransom, the Tennessee writer who established an important literary journal, the *Kenyon Review*. In contrast to Ransom's somewhat stark poem is a reminiscence of the circus by Thomas Wolfe, which rings with vibrant images and rich details. Following an excerpt from the classic Civil War novel *Gone With the Wind* are two stories by one of the South's most innovative and highly regarded writers, William Faulkner. Of these, one is a chilling example of the Southern gothic tradition, and the other a complex but riveting account of a stranger's destructive effect on a small Southern town.

Following the masterful writings of Faulkner is a group of selections about childhood. Carson McCullers' first short story, "Wunderkind," a poignant tale of a child prodigy, is followed by the opening chapter of James Still's *River of Earth*, a young boy's vivid description of Appalachian life. A story by Eudora Welty, about a frightening episode in a young girl's life, reveals this great writer's classically Southern talent for rendering grotesque characters in a sensitive way. A poem by Margaret Walker, recalling harsh images from childhood, and a short story by Jesse Stuart about a young boy's love for his ailing grandfather add other dimensions to this multifaceted look at Southern childhood.

Among the most recent selections in this anthology are two stories by Flannery O'Connor, a true master of the Southern gothic style who tempers her often shocking tales with humor. You'll also find two evocative poems by Georgian writer James Dickey, and a short story by Wendell Berry about the strong link that can exist between the present and the past. Before John Holman's concluding essay, you'll experience a powerful speech by Martin Luther King, Jr., delivered just a day before his assassination in 1968, and poem by Alice Walker about a special place in her hometown.

These works of fiction, nonfiction, and poetry are sure to draw you in and hold you fast. As you savor each selection, allow your senses to fully experience the rhythms, flavors, and feelings of the South.

from
Notes on Virginia

Thomas Jefferson

IN enumerating the defects of the Constitution, it would be wrong to count among them what is only the error of particular persons. In December 1776, our circumstances being much distressed, it was proposed in the house of delegates to create a *dictator,* invested with every power legislative, executive, and judiciary, civil and military, of life and of death, over our persons and over our properties; and in June 1781, again under calamity, the same proposition was repeated and wanted a few votes only of being passed. One who entered into this contest from a pure love of liberty, and a sense of injured rights, who determined to make every sacrifice, and to meet every danger, for the re-establishment of those rights on a firm basis, who did not mean to expend his blood and substance for the wretched purpose of changing this matter for that, but to place the powers of governing him in a plurality of hands of his own choice, so that the corrupt will of no one man might in future oppress him, must stand confounded and dismayed when he is told, that a considerable portion of that plurality had mediated the surrender of them into a single hand, and, in lieu of a limited monarchy, to deliver him over to a despotic one! How must we find his efforts and sacrifices abused and baffled, if he may still, by a single vote, be laid prostrate at the feet of one man! In God's name, from whence have they derived this power? Is it from our ancient laws? None such can be produced. Is it from any principle in our new Constitution expressed or implied? Every lineament expressed or implied, is in full opposition to it. Its fundamental principle is, that the State shall be governed as a commonwealth. It provides a republican organization, proscribes under the name of *prerogative* the exercise of all powers undefined by the laws; places on this basis the whole system of our laws; and by consolidating them together, chooses that they should be left to stand or fall together, never providing for any circumstances, nor admitting that such could arise, wherein either should be suspended; no, not for a moment. Our ancient

laws expressly declare, that those who are but delegates themselves shall not delegate to others powers which require judgment and integrity in their exercise. Or was this proposition
moved on a supposed right in the movers, of abandoning their
posts in a moment of distress? The same laws forbid the aban-
donment of that post, even on ordinary occasions; and much
more a transfer of their powers into other hands and other
forms, without consulting the people. They never admit the idea
that these, like sheep or cattle, may be given from hand to hand
without an appeal to their own will. Was it from the necessity of
the case? Necessities which dissolve a government, do not con-
vey its authority to an oligarchy or a monarchy. They throw
back, into the hands of the people, the powers they had dele-
gated, and leave them as individuals to shift for themselves. A
leader may offer, but not impose himself, nor be imposed on
them. Much less can their necks be submitted to his sword,
their breath to be held at his will or caprice. The necessity
which should operate these tremendous effects should at least
be palpable and irresistible. Yet in both instances, where it was
feared, or pretended with us, it was belied by the event. It was
belied, too, by the preceding experience of our sister States, several of whom had grappled through greater difficulties without
abandoning their forms of government. When the proposition
was first made, Massachusetts had found even the government
of committees sufficient to carry them through an invasion. But
we at the time of that proposition, were under no invasion.
When the second was made, there had been added to this example those of Rhode Island, New York, New Jersey, and Pennsylvania, in all of which the republican form had been found
equal to the task of carrying them through the severest trials. In
this State alone did there exist so little virtue, that fear was to
be fixed in the hearts of the people, and to become the motive of
their exertions, and principle of their government? The very
thought alone was treason against the people; was treason
against mankind in general; as riveting forever the chains which
bow down their necks, by giving to their oppressors a proof,
which they would have trumpeted through the universe, of the
imbecility of republican government, in times of pressing danger, to shield them from harm. Those who assume the right of
giving away the reins of government in any case, must be sure
that the herd, whom they hand on to the rods and hatchet of
the dictator, will lay their necks on the block when he shall nod

to them. But if our assemblies supposed such a recognition in the people, I hope they mistook their character. I am of opinion, that the government, instead of being braced and invigorated for greater exertions under their difficulties, would have been thrown back upon the bungling machinery of county committees for administration, till a convention could have been called, and its wheels again set into regular motion. What a cruel moment was this for creating such an embarrassment, for putting to the proof the attachment of our countrymen to republican government! Those who meant well, of the advocates of this measure, (and most of them meant well, for I know them personally, had been their fellow-laborer in the common cause, and had often proved the purity of their principles,) had been seduced in their judgment by the example of an ancient republic, whose constitution and circumstances were fundamentally different. They had sought this precedent in the history of Rome, where alone it was to be found, and where at length, too, it had proved fatal. They had taken it from a republic rent by the most bitter factions and tumults, where the government was of a heavy-handed unfeeling aristocracy, over a people ferocious, and rendered desperate by poverty and wretchedness; tumults which could not be allayed under the most trying circumstances, but by the omnipotent hand of a single despot. Their constitution, therefore, allowed a temporary tyrant to be erected, under the name of a dictator; and that temporary tyrant, after a few examples, became perpetual. They misapplied this precedent to a people mild in their dispositions, patient under their trial, united for the public liberty, and affectionate to their leaders.

• • •

The present state of our laws on the subject of religion is this. The convention of May 1776, in their declaration of rights, declared it to be a truth, and a natural right, that the exercise of religion should be free; but when they proceeded to form on that declaration the ordinance of government, instead of taking up every principle declared in the bill of rights, and guarding it by legislative sanction, they passed over that which asserted our religious rights, leaving them as they found them. The same convention, however, when they met as a member of the general assembly in October, 1776, repealed all *acts of Parliament* which had rendered criminal the maintaining any opinions in matters of religion, the forbearing to repair to church, and the exercising any mode of worship; and suspended the laws giving salaries to the clergy, which suspension was made perpetual in October, 1779. Statutory oppressions in religion being thus wiped away, we remain at present under those only imposed by the common law, or by our own acts of assembly. At the common law, *heresy* was a capital offence, punishable by burning. Its definition was left to the ecclesiastical judges, before whom the conviction was, till the statute of the 1 El. c. 1 circumscribed it, by declaring, that nothing should be deemed heresy, but what had been so determined by authority of the canonical scriptures, or by one of the four first general councils, or by other council, having for the grounds of their declaration the express and plain words of the scriptures. Heresy, thus circumscribed, being an offence against the common law, our act of assembly of October 1777, c. 17, gives cognizance of it to the general court, by declaring that the jurisdiction of that court shall be general in all matters at the common law. The execution is by the writ *De hoeretico comburendo.* By our own act of assembly of 1705, c. 30, if a person brought up in the Christian religion denies the being of a God, or the Trinity, or asserts there are more gods than one, or denies the Christian religion to be true, or the scriptures to be of divine authority, he is punishable on the first offence by incapacity to hold any office or employment ecclesiastical, civil, or military; on the second by disability to sue, to take any gift or legacy, to be guardian, executor, or administrator, and by three years' imprisonment without bail. A father's right to the custody of his own children being founded in law on his right of guardianship, this being taken away, they may of course be severed from him, and put by the authority of a court into more orthodox hands. This is a summary view of that religious slavery under which a people have been willing to remain, who have lavished their lives and fortunes for the establishment of their civil freedom. The error seems not sufficiently eradicated, that the operations of the mind, as well as the acts of the body, are subject to the coercion of the laws. But our rulers can have no authority over such natural rights, only as we have submitted to them. The rights of conscience we never submitted, we could not submit. We are answerable for them to our God. The legitimate powers of government extend to such acts only as are injurious to others. But it does me no injury for my neighbor to say there are twenty gods, or no God. It neither picks my pocket nor breaks my leg. If it be said, his testimony in a court of justice cannot be relied on, reject it then, and be the stigma on him. Constraint may make him worse by making him a hypocrite, but it will never make him a truer man. It may fix him obstinately in his errors, but will not cure them. Reason and free inquiry are the only effectual agents against error. Give a loose to them, they will support the true religion by bringing every false one to their tribunal, to the test of their investigation. They are the natural enemies of error, and of error only. Had not the Roman government permitted free inquiry, Christianity could never have been introduced. Had not free inquiry been indulged at the era of the Reformation, the corruptions of Christianity could not have been purged away. If it be restrained now, the present corruptions will be protected, and new ones encouraged. Was the government to prescribe to us our medicine and diet, our bodies would be in such keeping as our souls are now. Thus in France the emetic was once forbidden as a medicine, and the potato as an article of food. Government is just as infallible, too, when it fixes systems in physics. Galileo was sent to the Inquisition for affirming that the earth was a sphere; the government had declared it to be as flat as a trencher, and Galileo was obliged to abjure his error. This error, however, at length prevailed, the earth became a globe, and Descartes declared it was whirled round its axis by a vortex. The government in which he lived was wise enough to see that this was no question of civil jurisdiction, or we should all have been involved by authority in vortices. In fact, the vortices have been exploded, and the Newtonian principle of gravitation is now more firmly established, on the basis of reason, than it would be were the government to step in, and to make it an article of necessary faith. Reason and experiment have been indulged, and error has fled before them. It is error alone which needs the support of government. Truth can stand by itself. Subject opinion to coercion: whom will you make your inquisitors? Fallible men; men governed by bad passions, by private as well as public reasons. And why subject it to coercion? To produce uniformity. But is uniformity of opinion desirable? No more than of face and stature. Introduce the bed of Procrustes then, and as there is danger that the large men may beat the small, make us all of a size, by lopping the former and stretching the latter. Difference of opinion is advantageous in religion. The several sects perform the office of a *censor morum* over such other. Is uniformity attainable? Millions of innocent men, women, and children, since the introduction of Christianity, have been burnt, tortured, fined, imprisoned; yet we have not advanced one inch towards uniformity. What has been the effect of coercion? To make one half the world fools, and the other half hypocrites. To support roguery and error all over the earth. Let us reflect that it is inhabited by a thousand millions of people. That these profess probably a thousand different systems of religion. That ours is but one of that thousand. That if there be but one right, and ours that one, we should wish to see the nine hundred and ninety-nine wandering sects gathered into the fold of truth. But against such a majority we cannot effect this by force. Reason and persuasion are the only practicable instruments. To make way for these, free inquiry must be indulged; and how can we wish others to indulge it while we refuse it ourselves. But every State, says an inquisitor, has established some religion. No two, say I, have established the same. Is this a proof of the infallibility of establishments? Our sister States of Pennsylvania and New York, however, have long subsisted without any establishment at all. The experiment was new and doubtful when they made it. It has answered beyond conception. They flourish infinitely. Religion is well supported; of various kinds, indeed, but all good enough; all sufficient to preserve peace and order; or if a sect arises, whose tenets would subvert morals, good sense has fair play, and reasons and laughs it out of doors, without suffering the State to be troubled with it. They do not hang more malefactors than we do. They are not more disturbed with religious dissensions. On the contrary, their harmony is unparalleled, and can be ascribed to nothing but their unbounded tolerance, because there is no other circumstance in which they differ from every nation on earth. They have made the happy discovery, that the way to silence religious disputes, is to take no notice of them. Let us too give this experiment fair play, and get rid, while we may, of those tyrannical laws. It is true, we are as yet secured against them by the spirit of the times. I doubt whether the people of this country would suffer an execution for heresy, or a three years' imprisonment for not comprehending the mysteries of the Trinity. But is the spirit of the people an infallible, a permanent reliance? Is it government? Is this the kind of protection we receive in return for the rights we give up? Besides, the spirit of the times may alter, will alter. Our rulers will become corrupt, our people careless. A single zealot may commence persecutor, and better men be his victims. It can never be too often repeated, that the time for fixing every essential right on a legal basis is while our rulers are honest, and ourselves united. From the conclusion of this war we shall be going down hill. It will not then be necessary to resort every moment to the people for support. They will be forgotten, therefore, and their rights disregarded. They will forget themselves, but in the sole faculty of making money, and will never think of uniting to effect a due respect for their rights. The shackles, therefore, which shall not be knocked off at the conclusion of this war, will remain on us long, will be made heavier and heavier, till our rights shall revive or expire in a convulsion.

• • •

It is difficult to determine on the standard by which the manners of a nation may be tried, whether *catholic* or *particular*. It is more difficult for a native to bring to that standard the manners of his own nation, familiarized to him by habit. There must doubtless be an unhappy influence on the manners of our people produced by the existence of slavery among us. The whole commerce between master and slave is a perpetual exercise of the most boisterous passions, the most unremitting despotism on the one part, and degrading submissions on the other. Our children see this, and learn to imitate it; for man is an imitative animal. This quality is the germ of all education in him. From his cradle to his grave he is learning to do what he sees others do. If a parent could find no motive either in his philanthropy or his self-love, for restraining the intemperance of passion towards his slave, it should always be a sufficient one that his child is present. But generally it is not sufficient. The parent storms, the child looks on, catches the lineaments of wrath, puts on the same airs in the circle of smaller slaves, gives a loose to the worst of passions, and thus nursed, educated, and daily exercised in tyranny, cannot but be stamped by it with odious peculiarities. The man must be a prodigy who can retain his manners and morals undepraved by such circumstances. And with what execration should the statesman be loaded, who, permitting one half the citizens thus to trample on the rights of the other, transforms those into despots, and these into enemies, destroys the morals of the one part, and the *amor patriae* of the other. For if a slave can have a country in this world, it must be any other in preference to that in which he is born to live and labor for another; in which he must lock up the faculties of his nature, contribute as far as depends on his individual endeavors to the evanishment of the human race, or entail his own miserable condition on the endless generations proceeding from him. With the morals of the people, their industry also is destroyed. For in a warm climate, no man will labor for himself who can make another labor for him. This is so true, that of the proprietors of slaves a very small proportion indeed are ever seen to labor. And can the liberties of a nation be thought secure when we have removed their only firm basis, a conviction in the minds of the people that these liberties are of the gift of God? That they are not to be violated but with His wrath? Indeed I tremble for my country when I reflect that God is just; that his justice cannot sleep forever; that considering numbers, nature and natural means only, a revolution of the wheel of fortune, an exchange of situation is among possible events; that it may become probable by supernatural interference! The Almighty has no attribute which can take side with us in such a contest. But it is impossible to be temperate and to pursue this subject through the various considerations of policy, of morals, of history natural and civil. We must be contented to hope they will force their way into every one's mind. I think a change already perceptible, since the origin of the present revolution. The spirit of the master is abating, that of the slave rising from the dust, his condition mollifying, the way I hope preparing, under the auspices of heaven, for a total emancipation, and that this is disposed, in the order of events, to be with the consent of the master, rather than by their extirpation.

Ode on the Confederate Dead

Henry Timrod

SUNG AT THE OCCASION OF DECORATING
THE GRAVES AT MAGNOLIA CEMETERY,
CHARLESTON, S.C., 1867

Sleep sweetly in your humble graves,
   Sleep, martyrs of a fallen cause;
Though yet no marble column craves
   The pilgrim here to pause.

In seeds of laurel in the earth
   The blossom of your fame is blown,
And somewhere, waiting for its birth,
   The shaft is in the stone!

Meanwhile, behalf the tardy years
   Which keep in trust your storied tombs,
Behold! your sisters bring their tears,
   And these memorial blooms.

Small tributes! but your shades will smile
   More proudly on these wreaths today,
Than when some cannon-molded pile
   Shall overlook this bay.

Stoop, angels, hither from the skies!
   There is no holier spot of ground
Than where defeated valor lies,
   By mourning beauty crowned!

Song of the Chattahoochee

Sidney Lanier

Out of the hills of Habersham,
　　Down the valleys of Hall,
I hurry amain to reach the plain,
Run the rapid and leap the fall,
Split at the rock and together again,
Accept my bed, or narrow or wide,
And flee from folly on every side
With a lover's pain to attain the plain
　　　Far from the hills of Habersham,
　　　Far from the valleys of Hall.

All down the hills of Habersham,
　　All through the valleys of Hall,
The rushes cried *Abide, abide,*
The willful waterweeds held me thrall,
The laving laurel turned my tide,
The ferns and the fondling grass said *Stay,*
The dewberry dipped for to work delay,
And the little reeds sighed *Abide, abide,*
　　　Here in the hills of Habersham,
　　　Here in the valleys of Hall.

High o'er the hills of Habersham,
　　Veiling the valleys of Hall,
The hickory told me manifold
Fair tales of shade, the poplar tall
Wrought me her shadowy self to hold,
The chestnut, the oak, the walnut, the pine,
Overleaning, with flickering meaning and sign,

Said, *Pass not, so cold, these manifold*
  Deep shades of the hills of Habersham,
  These glades in the valleys of Hall.

  And oft in the hills of Habersham,
  And oft in the valleys of Hall,
The white quartz shone, and the smooth brook-stone
Did bar me of passage with friendly brawl,
And many a luminous jewel lone
—Crystals clear or a-cloud with mist,
Ruby, garnet and amethyst—
Made lures with the lights of streaming stone
  In the clefts of the hills of Habersham,
  In the beds of the valleys of Hall.

  But oh, not the hills of Habersham,
  And oh, not the valleys of Hall
Avail : I am fain for to water the plain.
Downward the voices of Duty call—
Downward, to toil and be mixed with the main,
The dry fields burn, and the mills are to turn,
And a myriad flowers mortally yearn,
And the lordly main from beyond the plain
  Calls o'er the hills of Habersham,
  Calls through the valleys of Hall.

The Marshes of Glynn

Sidney Lanier

Glooms of the live-oaks, beautiful-braided and woven
With intricate shades of the vines that myriad-cloven
    Clamber the forks of the multiform boughs,—
          Emerald twilights,—
          Virginal shy lights,
Wrought of the leaves to allure to the whisper of vows,
When lovers pace timidly down through the green colon-
    nades
Of the dim sweet woods, of the dear dark woods,
   Of the heavenly woods and glades,
That run to the radiant marginal sand-beach within
    The wide sea-marshes of Glynn;—

Beautiful glooms, soft dusks in the noon-day fire,—
Wildwood privacies, closets of lone desire,
Chamber from chamber parted with wavering arras of
    leaves,—
Cells for the passionate pleasure of prayer to the soul that
    grieves,
Pure with a sense of the passing of saints through the
    wood,
Cool for the dutiful weighing of ill with good;—

O braided dusks of the oak and woven shades of the vine,
While the riotous noon-day sun of the June-day long did
    shine
Ye held me fast in your heart and I held you fast in mine;

But now when the noon is no more, and riot is rest,
And the sun is a-wait at the ponderous gate of the West,
And the slant yellow beam down the wood-aisle doth seem
Like a lane into heaven that leads from a dream,—
Ay, now, when my soul all day hath drunken the soul of the
    oak,
And my heart is at ease from men, and the wearisome
    sound of the stroke
  Of the scythe of time and the trowel of trade is low,
    And belief overmasters doubt, and I know that I know,
    And my spirit is grown to a lordly great compass within,
That the length and the breadth and the sweep of the
    marshes of Glynn
Will work me no fear like the fear they have wrought me of
    yore
When length was fatigue, and when breadth was but bitter-
    ness sore,
And when terror and shrinking and dreary unnamable pain
Drew over me out of the merciless miles of the plain,—

Oh, now, unafraid, I am fain to face
  The vast sweet visage of space.
To the edge of the wood I am drawn, I am drawn,
Where the gray beach glimmering runs, as a belt of the
    dawn,
  For a mete and a mark
  To the forest-dark:—
       So:
Affable live-oak, leaning low,—
Thus—with your favor—soft, with a reverent hand,
(Not lightly touching your person, Lord of the land!)
Bending your beauty aside, with a step I stand
On the firm-packed sand,
      Free
By a world of marsh that borders a world of sea.
  Sinuous southward and sinuous northward the shimmer-
    ing band
  Of the sand-beach fastens the fringe of the marsh to the
    folds of the land.
Inward and outward to northward and southward the
    beachlines linger and curl

As a silver-wrought garment that clings to and follows the
    firm sweet limbs of a girl.
Vanishing, swerving, evermore curving again into sight,
Softly the sand-beach wavers away to a dim gray looping of
    light.
And what if behind me to westward the wall of the woods
    stands high?
The world lies east: how ample, the marsh and the sea and
    the sky!
A league and a league of marsh-grass, waist-high, broad in
    the blade,
Green, and all of a height, and unflecked with a light or a
    shade,
Stretch leisurely off, in a pleasant plain,
To the terminal blue of the main.

Oh, what is abroad in the marsh and the terminal sea?
    Somehow my soul seems suddenly free
From the weighing of fate and the sad discussion of sin,
By the length and the breadth and the sweep of the
    marshes of Glynn.

Ye marshes, how candid and simple and nothing-withhold-
    ing and free
Ye publish yourselves to the sky and offer yourselves to the
    sea!
Tolerant plains, that suffer the sea and the rains and the
    sun,
Ye spread and span like the catholic man who hath mightily
    won
God out of knowledge and good out of infinite pain
And sight out of blindness and purity out of a stain.

As the marsh-hen secretly builds on the watery sod,
Behold I will build me a nest on the greatness of God:
I will fly in the greatness of God as the marsh-hen flies
In the freedom that fills all the space 'twixt the marsh and
    the skies:
By so many roots as the marsh-grass sends in the sod
I will heartily lay me a-hold on the greatness of God:

Oh, like to the greatness of God is the greatness within
The range of the marshes, the liberal marshes of Glynn.

And the sea lends large, as the marsh: lo, out of his plenty
    the sea
Pours fast: full soon the time of the flood-tide must be:
Look how the grace of the sea doth go
About and about through the intricate channels that flow
    Here and there,
               Everywhere,
Till his waters have flooded the uttermost creeks and the
    low-lying lanes,
And the marsh is meshed with a million veins,
That like as with rosy and silvery essences flow
  In the rose-and-silver evening glow.
             Farewell, my lord Sun !
The creeks overflow: a thousand rivulets run
'Twixt the roots of the sod; the blades of the marsh-grass
    stir;
Passeth a hurrying sound of wings that westward whirr;
Passeth, and all is still; and the currents cease to run;
And the sea and the marsh are one.

How still the plains of the waters be !
The tide is in his ecstasy.
The tide is at his highest height:
        And it is night.

And now from the Vast of the Lord will the waters of sleep
Roll in on the souls of men,
But who will reveal to our waking ken
The forms that swim and the shapes that creep
       Under the waters of sleep?
And I would I could know what swimmeth below when the
    tide comes in
On the length and the breadth of the marvellous marshes of
    Glynn.

The Struggle for an Education

Booker T. Washington

ONE day, while at work in the coal-mine, I happened to overhear two miners talking about a great school for coloured people somewhere in Virginia. This was the first time that I had ever heard anything about any kind of school or college that was more pretentious than the little coloured school in our town.

In the darkness of the mine I noiselessly crept as close as I could to the two men who were talking. I heard one tell the other that not only was the school established for the members of my race, but that opportunities were provided by which poor but worthy students could work out all or a part of the cost of board, and at the same time be taught some trade or industry.

As they went on describing the school, it seemed to me that it must be the greatest place on earth, and not even Heaven presented more attractions for me at that time than did the Hampton Normal and Agricultural Institute in Virginia, about which these men were talking. I resolved at once to go to that school, although I had no idea where it was, or how many miles away, or how I was going to reach it; I remembered only that I was on fire constantly with one ambition, and that was to go to Hampton. This thought was with me day and night.

After hearing of the Hampton Institute, I continued to work for a few months longer in the coal-mine. While at work there, I heard of a vacant position in the household of General Lewis Ruffner, the owner of the salt-furnace and coal-mine. Mrs. Viola Ruffner, the wife of General Ruffner, was a "Yankee" woman from Vermont. Mrs. Ruffner had a reputation all through the vicinity for being very strict with her servants, and especially with the boys who tried to serve her. Few of them had remained with her more than two or three weeks. They all left with the same excuse: she was too strict. I decided, however, that I would rather try Mrs. Ruffner's house than remain in the coal-mine, and so my mother applied to her for the vacant position. I was hired at a salary of $5 per month.

I had heard so much about Mrs. Ruffner's severity that I was almost afraid to see her, and trembled when I went into her presence. I had not lived with her many weeks, however, before I began to understand her. I soon began to learn that, first of all, she wanted everything kept clean about her, that she wanted things done promptly and systematically, and that at the bottom of everything she wanted absolute honesty and frankness. Nothing must be sloven or slipshod; every door, every fence, must be kept in repair.

I cannot now recall how long I lived with Mrs. Ruffner before going to Hampton, but I think it must have been a year and a half. At any rate, I here repeat what I have said more than once before, that the lessons that I learned in the home of Mrs. Ruffner were as valuable to me as any education I have ever gotten anywhere since. Even to this day I never see bits of paper scattered around a house or in the street that I do not want to pick them up at once. I never see a filthy yard that I do not want to clean it, a paling off of a fence that I do not want to put it on, an unpainted or unwhitewashed house that I do not want to paint or whitewash it, or a button off one's clothes, or a grease-spot on them or on a floor, that I do not want to call attention to it.

From fearing Mrs. Ruffner I soon learned to look upon her as one of my best friends. When she found that she could trust me she did so implicitly. During the one or two winters that I was with her she gave me an opportunity to go to school for an hour in the day during a portion of the winter months, but most of my studying was done at night, sometimes alone, sometimes under some one whom I could hire to teach me. Mrs. Ruffner always encouraged and sympathized with me in all my efforts to get an education. It was while living with her that I began to get together my first library. I secured a dry-goods box, knocked out one side of it, put some shelves in it, and began putting into it every kind of book that I could get my hands upon, and called it my "library."

Notwithstanding my success at Mrs. Ruffner's I did not give up the idea of going to the Hampton Institute. In the fall of 1872 I determined to make an effort to get there, although, as I have stated, I had no definite idea of the direction in which Hampton was, or of what it would cost to go there. I do not think that any one thoroughly sympathized with me in my ambition to go to Hampton unless it was my mother, and she was troubled with a grave fear that I was starting out on a "wild-goose chase." At any rate, I got only a half-hearted consent from her that I might start. The small amount of money that I had earned had been consumed by my stepfather and the remainder of the family, with the exception of a very few dollars, and so I had very little with which to buy clothes and pay my travelling expenses. My brother John helped me all that he could, but of course that was not a great deal, for his work was in the coal-mine, where he did not earn much, and most of what he did earn went in the direction of paying the household expenses.

Perhaps the thing that touched and pleased me most in connection with my starting for Hampton was the interest that many of the older coloured people took in the matter. They had spent the best days of their lives in slavery, and hardly expected to live to see the time when they would see a member of their race leave home to attend a boarding-school. Some of these older people would give me a nickel, others a quarter, or a handkerchief.

Finally the great day came, and I started for Hampton. I had only a small, cheap satchel that contained what few articles of clothing I could get. My mother at the time was rather weak and broken in health. I hardly expected to see her again, and thus our parting was all the more sad. She, however, was very brave through it all. At that time there were no through trains connecting that part of West Virginia with eastern Virginia. Trains ran only a portion of the way, and the remainder of the distance was travelled by stage-coaches.

The distance from Malden to Hampton is about five hundred miles. I had not been away from home many hours before it began to grow painfully evident that I did not have enough money to pay my fare to Hampton. One experience I shall long remember. I had been travelling over the mountains most of the afternoon in an old-fashioned stage-coach, when, late in the evening, the coach stopped for the night at a common, unpainted house called a hotel. All the other passengers except myself were whites. In my ignorance I supposed that the little hotel existed for the purpose of accommodating the passengers who travelled on the stage-coach. The difference that the colour of one's skin would make I had not thought anything about. After all the other passengers had been shown rooms and were getting ready for supper, I shyly presented myself before the man at the desk. It is true I had practically no money in my pocket with which to pay for bed or food, but I had hoped in some way to beg my way into the good graces of the landlord, for at that season in the mountains of Virginia the weather was cold, and I wanted to get indoors for the night. Without asking as to whether I had any money, the man at the desk firmly refused to even consider the matter of providing me with food or lodging. This was my first experience in finding out what the colour of my skin meant. In some way I managed to keep warm by walking about, and so got through the night. My whole soul was so bent upon reaching Hampton that I did not have time to cherish any bitterness toward the hotel-keeper.

By walking, begging rides both in wagons and in the cars, in some way, after a number of days, I reached the city of Richmond, Virginia, about eighty-two miles from Hampton. When I reached there, tired, hungry, and dirty, it was late in the night. I had never been in a large city, and this rather added to my misery. When I reached Richmond, I was completely out of money. I had not a single acquaintance in the place, and, being unused to city ways, I did not know where to go. I applied at several places for lodging, but they all wanted money, and that was what I did not have. Knowing nothing else better to do, I walked the streets. In doing this I passed by many food-stands where fried chicken and half-moon apple pies were piled high and made to present a most tempting appearance. At that time it seemed to me that I would have promised all that I expected to possess in the future to have gotten hold of one of those chicken legs or one of those pies. But I could not get either of these, nor anything else to eat.

I must have walked the streets till after midnight. At last I became so exhausted that I could walk no longer. I was tired, I was hungry, I was everything but discouraged. Just about the time when I reached extreme physical exhaustion, I came upon a portion of a street where the board sidewalk was considerably elevated. I waited for a few minutes, till I was sure that no passers-by could see me, and then crept under the sidewalk and lay for the night upon the ground, with my satchel of clothing for a pillow. Nearly all night I could hear the tramp of feet over my head. The next morning I found myself somewhat refreshed, but I was extremely hungry, because it had been a long time since I had had sufficient food. As soon as it became light enough for me to see my surroundings I noticed that I was near a large ship, and that this ship seemed to be unloading a cargo of pig iron. I went at once to the vessel and asked the captain to permit me to help unload the vessel in order to get money for food. The captain, a white man, who seemed to be kind-hearted, consented. I worked long enough to earn money for my breakfast, and it seems to me, as I remember it now, to have been about the best breakfast that I have ever eaten.

My work pleased the captain so well that he told me if I desired I could continue working for a small amount per day. This I was very glad to do. I continued working on this vessel for a number of days. After buying food with the small wages I received there was not much left to add to the amount I must get to pay my way to Hampton. In order to economize in every way possible, so as to be sure to reach Hampton in a reasonable time, I continued to sleep under the same sidewalk that gave me shelter the first night I was in Richmond. Many years after that the coloured citizens of Richmond very kindly tendered me a reception at which there must have been two thousand people present. This reception was held not far from the spot where I slept the first night I spent in that city, and I must confess that my mind was more upon the sidewalk that first gave me shelter than upon the reception, agreeable and cordial as it was.

When I had saved what I considered enough money with which to reach Hampton, I thanked the captain of the vessel for his kindness, and started again. Without any unusual occurrence I reached Hampton, with a surplus of exactly fifty cents with which to begin my education. To me it had been a long, eventful journey; but the first sight of the large, three-story, brick school building seemed to have rewarded me for all that I had undergone in order to reach the place. If the people who gave the money to provide that building could appreciate the influence the sight of it had upon me, as well as upon thousands of other youths, they would feel all the more encouraged to make such gifts. It seemed to me to be the largest and most beautiful building I had ever seen. The sight of it seemed to give me new life. I felt that a new kind of existence had now begun— that life would now have a new meaning. I felt that I had reached the promised land, and I resolved to let no obstacle prevent me from putting forth the highest effort to fit myself to accomplish the most good in the world.

As soon as possible after reaching the grounds of the Hampton Institute, I presented myself before the head teacher for assignment to a class. Having been so long without proper food, a bath, and change of clothing, I did not, of course, make a very favourable impression upon her, and I could see at once that there were doubts in her mind about the wisdom of admitting me as a student. I felt that I could hardly blame her if she got the idea that I was a worthless loafer or tramp. For some time she did not refuse to admit me, neither did she decide in my favour, and I continued to linger about her, and to impress her in all the ways I could with my worthiness. In the meantime I saw her admitting other students, and that added greatly to my discomfort, for I felt, deep down in my heart, that I could do as well as they, if I could only get a chance to show what was in me.

After some hours had passed, the head teacher said to me: "The adjoining recitation-room needs sweeping. Take the broom and sweep it."

It occurred to me at once that here was my chance. Never did I receive an order with more delight. I knew that I could sweep, for Mrs. Ruffner had thoroughly taught me how to do that when I lived with her.

I swept the recitation-room three times. Then I got a dusting-cloth and I dusted it four times. All the woodwork around the walls, every bench, table, and desk, I went over four times with my dusting-cloth. Besides, every piece of furniture had been moved and every closet and corner in the room had been thoroughly cleaned. I had the feeling that in a large measure my future depended upon the impression I made upon the teacher in the cleaning of that room. When I was through, I reported to the head teacher. She was a "Yankee" woman who knew just where to look for dirt. She went into the room and inspected the floor and closets; then she took her handkerchief and rubbed it on the woodwork about the walls, and over the table and benches. When she was unable to find one bit of dirt on the floor, or a particle of dust on any of the furniture, she quietly remarked, "I guess you will do to enter this institution."

I was one of the happiest souls on earth. The sweeping of that room was my college examination, and never did any youth pass an examination for entrance into Harvard or Yale that gave him more genuine satisfaction. I have passed several examinations since then, but I have always felt that this was the best one I ever passed.

• • •

When I first went to Hampton I do not recall that I had ever slept in a bed that had two sheets on it. In those days there were not many buildings there, and room was very precious. There were seven other boys in the same room with me; most of them, however, students who had been there for some time. The sheets were quite a puzzle to me. The first night I slept under both of them, and the second night I slept on top of both of them; but by watching the other boys I learned my lesson in this, and have been trying to follow it ever since and to teach it to others.

I was among the youngest of the students who were in Hampton at that time. Most of the students were men and women—some as old as forty years of age. As I now recall the scene of my first year, I do not believe that one often has the opportunity of coming into contact with three or four hundred men and women who were so tremendously in earnest as these men and women were. Every hour was occupied in study or work. Nearly all had had enough actual contact with the world to teach them the need of education. Many of the older ones were, of course, too old to master the text-books very thoroughly, and it was often sad to watch their struggles; but they made up in earnestness much of what they lacked in books. Many of them were as poor as I was, and, besides having to wrestle with their books, they had to struggle with a poverty which prevented their having the necessities of life. Many of them had aged parents who were dependent upon them, and some of them were men who had wives whose support in some way they had to provide for.

The great and prevailing idea that seemed to take possession of every one was to prepare himself to lift up the people at his home. No one seemed to think of himself. And the officers and teachers, what a rare set of human beings they were! They worked for the students night and day, in season and out of season. They seemed happy only when they were helping the students in some manner. Whenever it is written—and I hope it will be—the part that the Yankee teachers played in the education of the Negroes immediately after the war will make one of the most thrilling parts of the history of this country. The time is not far distant when the whole South will appreciate this service in a way that it has not yet been able to do.

Janet Waking

John Crowe Ransom

Beautifully Janet slept
Till it was deeply morning. She woke then
And thought about her dainty-feathered hen,
To see how it had kept.

One kiss she gave her mother.
Only a small one gave she to her daddy
Who would have kissed each curl of his shining baby;
No kiss at all for her brother.

"Old Chucky, old Chucky!" she cried,
Running across the world upon the grass
To Chucky's house, and listening. But alas,
Her Chucky had died.

It was a transmogrifying bee
Came droning down on Chucky's old bald head
And sat and put the poison. It scarcely bled,
But how exceedingly

And purply did the knot
Swell with the venom and communicate
Its rigor! Now the poor comb stood up straight
But Chucky did not.

So there was Janet
Kneeling on the wet grass, crying her brown hen
(Translated far beyond the daughters of men)
To rise and walk upon it.

And weeping fast as she had breath
Janet implored us, "Wake her from her sleep!"
And would not be instructed in how deep
Was the forgetful kingdom of death.

Circus at Dawn

Thomas Wolfe

THERE were times in early autumn—in September—when the greater circuses would come to town—the Ringling Brothers, Robinson's, and Barnum and Bailey shows, and when I was a route-boy on the morning paper, on those mornings when the circus would be coming in I would rush madly through my route in the cool and thrilling darkness that comes just before break of day, and then I would go back home and get my brother out of bed.

Talking in low excited voices we would walk rapidly back toward town under the rustle of September leaves, in cool streets just grayed now with that still, that unearthly and magical first light of day which seems suddenly to re-discover the great earth out of darkness, so that the earth emerges with an awful, a glorious sculptural stillness, and one looks out with a feeling of joy and disbelief, as the first men on this earth must have done, for to see this happen is one of the things that men will remember out of life forever and think of as they die.

At the sculptural still square where at one corner, just emerging into light, my father's shabby little marble shop stood with a ghostly strangeness and familiarity, my brother and I would "catch" the first street-car of the day bound for the "depot" where the circus was—or sometimes we would meet some one we knew, who would give us a lift in his automobile.

Then, having reached the dingy, grimy, and rickety depot section, we would get out, and walk rapidly across the tracks of the station yard, where we could see great flares and steamings from the engines, and hear the crash and bump of shifting freight cars, the swift sporadic thunders of a shifting engine, the tolling of bells, the sounds of great trains on the rails.

And to all these familiar sounds, filled with their exultant prophecies of flight, the voyage, morning, and the shining cities—to all the sharp and thrilling odors of the trains—the smell of cinders, acrid smoke, of musty, rusty freight cars, the clean pine-board of crated produce, and the smells of fresh stored food—oranges, coffee, tangerines and bacon, ham and flour and beef—there would be added now, with an unforgettable magic and familiarity, all the strange sounds and smells of the coming circus.

The gay yellow sumptuous-looking cars in which the star performers lived and slept, still dark and silent, heavily and powerfully still, would be drawn up in long strings upon the tracks. And all around them the sounds of the unloading circus would go on furiously in the darkness. The receding gulf of lilac and departing night would be filled with the savage roar of the lions, the murderously sudden snarling of great jungle cats, the trumpeting of the elephants, the stamp of the horses, and with the musty, pungent, unfamiliar odor of the jungle animals: the tawny camel smells, and the smells of panthers, zebras, tigers, elephants, and bears.

Then, along the tracks, beside the circus trains, there would be the sharp cries and oaths of the circus men, the magical swinging dance of lanterns in the darkness, the sudden heavy rumble of the loaded vans and wagons as they were pulled along the flats and gondolas, and down the runways to the ground. And everywhere, in the thrilling mystery of darkness and awakening light, there would be the tremendous conflict of a confused, hurried, and yet orderly movement.

The great iron-gray horses, four and six to a team, would be plodding along the road of thick white dust to a rattling of chains and traces and the harsh cries of their drivers. The men would drive the animals to the river which flowed by beyond the tracks, and water them; and as first light came one could see the elephants wallowing in the familiar river and the big horses going slowly and carefully down to drink.

Then, on the circus grounds, the tents were going up already with the magic speed of dreams. All over the place (which was near the tracks and the only space of flat land in the town that was big enough to hold a circus) there would be this fierce, savagely hurried, and yet orderly confusion. Great flares of gaseous circus light would blaze down on the seared and battered faces of the circus toughs as, with the rhythmic precision of a single animal—a human riveting machine—they swung their sledges at the stakes, driving a stake into the earth with the incredible instancy of accelerated figures in a motion picture. And everywhere, as light came, and the sun appeared, there would be a scene of magic, order, and of violence. The drivers would curse and talk their special language to their teams, there would be the loud, gasping and uneven labor of a gasoline engine, the shouts and curses of the bosses, the wooden riveting of driven stakes, and the rattle of heavy chains.

Already in an immense cleared space of dusty beaten earth, the stakes were being driven for the main exhibition tent. And an elephant would lurch ponderously to the field, slowly lower his great swinging head at the command of a man who sat perched upon his skull, flourish his gray wrinkled snout a time or two, and then solemnly wrap it around a tent pole big as the mast of a racing schooner. Then the elephant would back slowly away, dragging the great pole with him as if it were a stick of match-wood.

And when this happened, my brother would break into his great "whah-whah" of exuberant laughter, and prod me in the ribs with his clumsy fingers. And further on, two town darkeys, who had watched the elephant's performance with bulging eyes, would turn to each other with ape-like grins, bend double as they slapped their knees and howled with swart rich nigger-laughter, saying to each other in a kind of rhythmical chorus of question and reply:

"He don't play with it, do he?"

"No, *suh!* He don't send no boy!"

"He don't say 'Wait a minute,' do he?"

"No, suh! He say 'Come with me!' That's what he say!"

"He go boogety—boogety!" said one, suiting the words with a prowling movement of his black face toward the earth.

"He go rootin' faw it!" said the other, making a rooting movement with his head.

"He say 'Ar-rumpf!'" said one.

"He say 'Big boy, we is on ouah way'!" the other answered.

"Har! Har! Har! Har! Har!"—and they choked and screamed with their rich laughter, slapping their thighs with a solid smack as they described to each other the elephant's prowess.

Meanwhile, the circus food-tent—a huge canvas top without concealing sides—had already been put up, and now we could see the performers seated at long trestled tables underneath the tent, as they ate breakfast. And the savor of the food they ate— mixed as it was with our strong excitement, with the powerful but wholesome smells of the animals, and with all the joy, sweetness, mystery, jubilant magic and glory of the morning and the coming of the circus—seemed to us to be of the most maddening and appetizing succulence of any food that we had ever known or eaten.

We could see the circus performers eating tremendous breakfasts, with all the savage relish of their power and strength: they ate big fried steaks, pork chops, rashers of bacon, a half dozen eggs, great slabs of fried ham and great stacks of wheat-cakes which a cook kept flipping in the air with the skill of a juggler, and which a husky-looking waitress kept rushing to their tables on loaded trays held high and balanced marvellously on the fingers of a brawny hand. And above all the maddening odors of the wholesome and succulent food, there brooded forever the sultry and delicious fragrance—that somehow seemed to add a zest and sharpness to all the powerful and thrilling life of morning—of strong boiling coffee, which we could see sending off clouds of steam from an enormous polished urn, and which the circus performers gulped down, cup after cup.

And the circus men and women themselves—these star performers—were such fine-looking people, strong and handsome, yet speaking and moving with an almost stern dignity and decorum, that their lives seemed to us to be as splendid and wonderful as any lives on earth could be. There was never anything loose, rowdy, or tough in their comportment, nor did the circus women look like painted whores, or behave indecently with the men.

Rather, these people in an astonishing way seemed to have created an established community which lived an ordered existence on wheels, and to observe with a stern fidelity unknown in towns and cities the decencies of family life. There would be a powerful young man, a handsome and magnificent young woman with blonde hair and the figure of an Amazon, and a powerfully-built, thick-set man of middle age, who had a stern, lined, responsible-looking face and a bald head. They were probably the members of a trapeze team—the young man and woman would leap through space like projectiles, meeting the grip of the older man and hurling back again upon their narrow perches, catching the swing of their trapeze in mid-air, and whirling thrice before they caught it, in a perilous and beautiful exhibition of human balance and precision.

But when they came into the breakfast tent, they would speak gravely yet courteously to other performers, and seat themselves in a family group at one of the long tables, eating their tremendous breakfasts with an earnest concentration, seldom speaking to one another, and then gravely, seriously and briefly.

And my brother and I would look at them with fascinated eyes: my brother would watch the man with the bald head for a while and then turn toward me, whispering:

"D-d-do you see that f-f-fellow there with the bald head? W-w-well he's the heavy man," he whispered knowingly. "He's the one that c-c-c-catches them! That f-f-fellow's got to know his business! You know what happens if he m-m-misses, don't you!" said my brother.

"What?" I would say in a fascinated tone.

My brother snapped his fingers in the air.

"Over!" he said. "D-d-done for! W-w-why, they'd be d-d-d-dead before they knew what happened. Sure!" he said, nodding vigorously. "It's a f-f-f-fact! If he ever m-m-m-misses it's all over! That boy has g-g-g-got to know his s-s-s-stuff!" my brother said. "W-w-w-why," he went on in a low tone of solemn conviction, "it w-w-w-wouldn't surprise me at all if they p-p-p-pay him s-s-seventy-five or a hundred dollars a week! It's a fact!" my brother cried vigorously.

And we would turn our fascinated stares again upon these splendid and romantic creatures, whose lives were so different from our own, and whom we seemed to know with such familiar and affectionate intimacy. And at length, reluctantly, with full light come and the sun up, we would leave the circus grounds and start for home.

And somehow the memory of all we had seen and heard that glorious morning, and the memory of the food-tent with its wonderful smells, would waken in us the pangs of such a ravenous hunger that we could not wait until we got home to eat. We would stop off in town at lunch-rooms and, seated on tall stools before the counter, we would devour ham-and-egg sandwiches, hot hamburgers red and pungent at their cores with coarse spicy sanguinary beef, coffee, glasses of foaming milk and doughnuts, and then go home to eat up everything in sight upon the breakfast table.

from
Gone With the Wind

Margaret Mitchell

SHE looked from the alcove into the huge drawing room and watched the dancers, remembering how beautiful this room had been when first she came to Atlanta during the war. Then the hardwood floors had shone like glass, and overhead the chandelier with its hundreds of tiny prisms had caught and reflected every ray of the dozens of candles it bore, flinging them, like gleams from diamonds, flame and sapphire about the room. The old portraits on the walls had been dignified and gracious and had looked down upon guests with an air of mellowed hospitality. The rosewood sofas had been soft and inviting and one of them, the largest, had stood in the place of honor in this same alcove where she now sat. It had been Scarlett's favorite seat at parties. From this point stretched the pleasant vista of drawing room and dining room beyond, the oval mahogany table which seated twenty and the twenty slim-legged chairs demurely against the walls, the massive sideboard and buffet weighted with heavy silver, with seven-branched candlesticks, goblets, cruets, decanters and shining little glasses. Scarlett had sat on that sofa so often in the first years of the war, always with some handsome officer beside her, and listened to violin and bull fiddle, accordion and banjo, and heard the exciting swishing noises which dancing feet made on the waxed and polished floor.

Now the chandelier hung dark. It was twisted askew and most of the prisms were broken, as if the Yankee occupants had made their beauty a target for their boots. Now an oil lamp and a few candles lighted the room and the roaring fire in the wide hearth gave most of the illumination. Its flickering light showed how irreparably scarred and splintered the dull old floor was. Squares on the faded paper on the wall gave evidence that once the portraits had hung there, and wide cracks in the plaster recalled the day during the siege when a shell had exploded on the house and torn off parts of the roof and second floor. The heavy old mahogany table, spread with cake and decanters, still presided in the empty-looking dining room but it was scratched and the broken legs showed signs of clumsy repair. The sideboard, the silver and the spindly chairs were gone. The dull-gold damask draperies which had covered the arching French windows at the back of the room were missing, and only the remnants of the lace curtains remained, clean but obviously mended.

In place of the curved sofa she had liked so much was a hard bench that was none too comfortable. She sat upon it with as good grace as possible, wishing her skirts were in such condition that she could dance. It would be so good to dance again. But, of course, she could do more with Frank in this sequestered alcove than in a breathless reel and she could listen fascinated to his talk and encourage him to greater flights of foolishness.

But the music certainly was inviting. Her slipper patted longingly in time with old Levi's large splayed foot as he twanged a strident banjo and called the figures of the reel. Feet swished and scraped and patted as the twin lines danced toward each other, retreated, whirled and made arches of their arms.

> "'Ole Dan Tucker he got drunk—'
> (Swing yo' padners!)
> 'Fell in de fiah an' he kick up a chunk!'
> (Skip light, light ladies!)"

After the dull and exhausting months at Tara it was good to hear music again and the sound of dancing feet, good to see familiar friendly faces laughing in the feeble light, calling old jokes and catchwords, bantering, rallying, coquetting. It was like coming to life again after being dead. It almost seemed that the bright days of five years ago had come back again. If she could close her eyes and not see the worn made-over dresses and the patched boots and mended slippers, if her mind did not call up the faces of boys missing from the reel, she might almost think that nothing had changed. But as she looked, watching the old men grouped about the decanter in the dining room, the matrons lining the walls, talking behind fanless hands, and the swaying, skipping young dancers, it came to her suddenly, coldly, frighteningly that it was all as greatly changed as if these familiar figures were ghosts.

They looked the same but they were different. What was it? Was it only that they were five years older? No, it was something more than the passing of time. Something had gone out of them, out of their world. Five years ago, a feeling of security had wrapped them all around so gently they were not even aware of it. In its shelter they had flowered. Now it was gone and with it had gone the old thrill, the old sense of something delightful and exciting just around the corner, the old glamor of their way of living.

She knew she had changed too, but not as they had changed, and it puzzled her. She sat and watched them and she felt herself an alien among them, as alien and lonely as if she had come from another world, speaking a language they did not understand and she not understanding theirs. Then she knew that this feeling was the same one she felt with Ashley. With him and with people of his kind—and they made up most of her world—she felt outside of something she could not understand.

Their faces were little changed and their manners not at all but it seemed to her that these two things were all that remained of her old friends. An ageless dignity, a timeless gallantry still clung about them and would cling until they died but they would carry undying bitterness to their graves, a bitterness too deep for words. They were a soft-spoken fierce, tired people who were defeated and would not know defeat, broken yet standing determinedly erect. They were crushed and helpless, citizens of conquered provinces. They were looking on the state they loved, seeing it trampled by the enemy, rascals making a mock of the law, their former slaves a menace, their men disfranchised, their women insulted. And they were remembering graves.

Everything in their old world had changed but the old forms. The old usages went on, must go on, for the forms were all that were left to them. They were holding tightly to the things they knew best and loved best in the old days, the leisured manners, the courtesy, the pleasant casualness in human contacts and, most of all, the protecting attitude of the men toward their women. True to the tradition in which they had been reared, the men were courteous and tender and they almost succeeded in creating an atmosphere of sheltering their women from all that was harsh and unfit for feminine eyes. That, thought Scarlett, was the height of absurdity, for there was little, now, which even the most cloistered women had not seen and known in the last five years. They had nursed the wounded, closed dying eyes, suffered war and fire and devastation, known terror and flight and starvation.

But, no matter what sights they had seen, what menial tasks they had done and would have to do, they remained ladies and gentlemen, royalty in exile—bitter, aloof, incurious, kind to one another, diamond hard, as bright and brittle as the crystals of the broken chandelier over their heads. The old days had gone but these people would go their ways as if the old days still existed, charming, leisurely, determined not to rush and scramble for pennies as the Yankees did, determined to part with none of the old ways.

Scarlett knew that she, too, was greatly changed. Otherwise she could not have done the things she had done since she was last in Atlanta; otherwise she would not now be contemplating doing what she desperately hoped to do. But there was a difference in their hardness and hers and just what the difference was, she could not, for the moment, tell. Perhaps it was that there was nothing she would not do, and there were so many things these people would rather die than do. Perhaps it was that they were without hope but still smiling at life, bowing gracefully and passing it by. And this Scarlett could not do.

She could not ignore life. She had to live it and it was too brutal, too hostile, for her even to try to gloss over its harshness with a smile. Of the sweetness and courage and unyielding pride of her friends, Scarlett saw nothing. She saw only a silly stiff-neckedness which observed facts but smiled and refused to look them in the face.

As she stared at the dancers, flushed from the reel, she wondered if things drove them as she was driven, dead lovers, maimed husbands, children who were hungry, acres slipping away, beloved roofs that sheltered strangers. But, of course, they were driven! She knew their circumstances only a little less thoroughly than she knew her own. Their losses had been her losses, their privations her privations, their problems her same problems. Yet they had reacted differently to them. The faces she was seeing in the room were not faces; they were masks, excellent masks which would never drop.

But if they were suffering as acutely from brutal circumstances as she was—and they were—how could they maintain this air of gaiety and lightness of heart? Why, indeed, should they even try to do it? They were beyond her comprehension and vaguely irritating. She couldn't be like them. She couldn't survey the wreck of the world with an air of casual unconcern. She was as hunted as a fox, running with a bursting heart, trying to reach a burrow before the hounds caught up.

Suddenly she hated them all because they were different from her, because they carried their losses with an air that she could never attain, would never wish to attain. She hated them, these smiling, light-footed strangers, these proud fools who took pride in something they had lost, seeming to be proud that they had lost it. The women bore themselves like ladies and she knew they were ladies, though menial tasks were their daily lot and they didn't know where their next dress was coming from. Ladies all! But she could not feel herself a lady, for all her velvet dress and scented hair, for all the pride of birth that stood behind her and the pride of wealth that had once been hers. Harsh contact with the red earth of Tara had stripped gentility from her and she knew she would never feel like a lady again until her table was weighted with silver and crystal and smoking with rich food, until her own horses and carriages stood in her stables, until black hands and not white took the cotton from Tara.

A Rose for Emily

William Faulkner

I

WHEN Miss Emily Grierson died, our whole town went to her funeral: the men through a sort of respectful affection for a fallen monument, the women mostly out of curiosity to see the inside of her house, which no one save an old manservant—a combined gardener and cook—had seen in at least ten years.

It was a big, squarish frame house that had once been white, decorated with cupolas and spires and scrolled balconies in the heavily lightsome style of the seventies, set on what had once been our most select street. But garages and cotton gins had encroached and obliterated even the august names of that neighborhood; only Miss Emily's house was left, lifting its stubborn and coquettish decay above the cotton wagons and the gasoline pumps—an eyesore among eyesores. And now Miss Emily had gone to join the representatives of those august names where they lay in the cedar-bemused cemetery among the ranked and anonymous graves of Union and Confederate soldiers who fell at the battle of Jefferson.

Alive, Miss Emily had been a tradition, a duty, and a care; a sort of hereditary obligation upon the town, dating from that day in 1894 when Colonel Sartoris, the mayor—he who fathered the edict that no Negro woman should appear on the streets without an apron—remitted her taxes, the dispensation dating from the death of her father on into perpetuity. Not that Miss Emily would have accepted charity. Colonel Sartoris invented an involved tale to the effect that Miss Emily's father had loaned money to the town, which the town, as a matter of business, preferred this way of repaying. Only a man of Colonel Sartoris' generation and thought could have invented it, and only a woman could have believed it.

When the next generation, with its more modern ideas, became mayors and aldermen, this arrangement created some little dissatisfaction. On the first of the year they mailed her a tax

notice. February came, and there was no reply. They wrote her
a formal letter, asking her to call at the sheriff's office at her
convenience. A week later the mayor wrote her himself, offering
to call or to send his car for her, and received in reply a note on
paper of an archaic shape, in a thin, flowing calligraphy in faded
ink, to the effect that she no longer went out at all. The tax notice was also enclosed, without comment.

They called a special meeting of the Board of Aldermen. A
deputation waited upon her, knocked at the door through which
no visitor had passed since she ceased giving china-painting
lessons eight or ten years earlier. They were admitted by the old
Negro into a dim hall from which a stairway mounted into still
more shadow. It smelled of dust and disuse—a close, dank
smell. The Negro led them into the parlor. It was furnished in
heavy, leather-covered furniture. When the Negro opened the
blinds of one window, they could see that the leather was
cracked; and when they sat down, a faint dust rose sluggishly
about their thighs, spinning with slow motes in the single sun-
ray. On a tarnished gilt easel before the fireplace stood a crayon
portrait of Miss Emily's father.

They rose when she entered—a small, fat woman in black,
with a thin gold chain descending to her waist and vanishing
into her belt, leaning on an ebony cane with a tarnished gold
head. Her skeleton was small and spare; perhaps that was why
what would have been merely plumpness in another was obesity
in her. She looked bloated, like a body long submerged in motionless water, and of that pallid hue. Her eyes, lost in the fatty
ridges of her face, looked like two small pieces of coal pressed
into a lump of dough as they moved from one face to another
while the visitors stated their errand.

She did not ask them to sit. She just stood in the door and
listened quietly until the spokesman came to a stumbling halt.
Then they could hear the invisible watch ticking at the end of
the gold chain.

Her voice was dry and cold. "I have no taxes in Jefferson.
Colonel Sartoris explained it to me. Perhaps one of you can gain
access to the city records and satisfy yourselves."

"But we have. We are the city authorities, Miss Emily.
Didn't you get a notice from the sheriff, signed by him?"

"I received a paper, yes," Miss Emily said. "Perhaps he consid-
ers himself the sheriff . . . I have no taxes in Jefferson."

"But there is nothing on the books to show that, you see. We must go by the—"

"See Colonel Sartoris. I have no taxes in Jefferson."

"But, Miss Emily—"

"See Colonel Sartoris." (Colonel Sartoris had been dead almost ten years.) "I have no taxes in Jefferson. Tobe!" The Negro appeared. "Show these gentlemen out."

II

SO she vanquished them, horse and foot, just as she had vanquished their fathers thirty years before about the smell. That was two years after her father's death and a short time after her sweetheart—the one we believed would marry her— had deserted her. After her father's death she went out very little; after her sweetheart went away, people hardly saw her at all. A few of the ladies had the temerity to call, but were not received, and the only sign of life about the place was the Negro man—a young man then—going in and out with a market basket.

"Just as if a man—any man—could keep a kitchen properly," the ladies said; so they were not surprised when the smell developed. It was another link between the gross, teeming world and the high and mighty Griersons.

A neighbor, a woman, complained to the mayor, Judge Stevens, eighty years old.

"But what will you have me do about it, madam?" he said.

"Why, send her word to stop it," the woman said. "Isn't there a law?"

"I'm sure that won't be necessary," Judge Stevens said. "It's probably just a snake or a rat that nigger of hers killed in the yard. I'll speak to him about it."

The next day he received two more complaints, one from a man who came in diffident deprecation. "We really must do something about it, Judge. I'd be the last one in the world to bother Miss Emily, but we've got to do something." That night the Board of Aldermen met—three graybeards and one younger man, a member of the rising generation.

"It's simple enough," he said. "Send her word to have her place cleaned up. Give her a certain time to do it in, and if she don't . . ."

"Dammit, sir," Judge Stevens said, "will you accuse a lady to her face of smelling bad?"

So the next night, after midnight, four men crossed Miss Emily's lawn and slunk about the house like burglars, sniffing along the base of the brickwork and at the cellar openings while one of them performed a regular sowing motion with his hand out of a sack slung from his shoulder. They broke open the cellar door and sprinkled lime there, and in all the out-buildings. As they recrossed the lawn, a window that had been dark was lighted and Miss Emily sat in it, the light behind her, and her upright torso motionless as that of an idol. They crept quietly across the lawn and into the shadow of the locusts that lined the street. After a week or two the smell went away.

That was when people had begun to feel really sorry for her. People in our town, remembering how old lady Wyatt, her great-aunt, had gone completely crazy at last, believed that the Griersons held themselves a little too high for what they really were. None of the young men were quite good enough for Miss Emily and such. We had long thought of them as a tableau, Miss Emily a slender figure in white in the background, her father a spraddled silhouette in the foreground, his back to her and clutching a horsewhip, the two of them framed by the back-flung front door. So when she got to be thirty and was still single, we were not pleased exactly, but vindicated; even with insanity in the family she wouldn't have turned down all of her chances if they had really materialized.

When her father died, it got about that the house was all that was left to her; and in a way, people were glad. At last they could pity Miss Emily. Being left alone, and a pauper, she had become humanized. Now she too would know the old thrill and the old despair of a penny more or less.

The day after his death all the ladies prepared to call at the house and offer condolence and aid, as is our custom. Miss Emily met them at the door, dressed as usual and with no trace of grief on her face. She told them that her father was not dead. She did that for three days, with the ministers calling on her, and the doctors, trying to persuade her to let them dispose of the body. Just as they were about to resort to law and force, she broke down, and they buried her father quickly.

We did not say she was crazy then. We believed she had to do that. We remembered all the young men her father had driven away, and we knew that with nothing left, she would have to cling to that which had robbed her, as people will.

III

SHE was sick for a long time. When we saw her again, her hair was cut short, making her look like a girl, with a vague resemblance to those angels in colored church windows—sort of tragic and serene.

The town had just let the contracts for paving the sidewalks, and in the summer after her father's death they began the work. The construction company came with niggers and mules and machinery, and a foreman named Homer Barron, a Yankee—a big, dark, ready man, with a big voice and eyes lighter than his face. The little boys would follow in groups to hear him cuss the niggers, and the niggers singing in time to the rise and fall of picks. Pretty soon he knew everybody in town. Whenever you heard a lot of laughing anywhere about the square, Homer Barron would be in the center of the group. Presently we began to see him and Miss Emily on Sunday afternoons driving in the yellow-wheeled buggy and the matched team of bays from the livery stable.

At first we were glad that Miss Emily would have an interest, because the ladies all said, "Of course a Grierson would not think seriously of a Northerner, a day laborer." But there was still others, older people, who said that even grief could not cause a real lady to forget *noblesse oblige*—without calling it *noblesse oblige.* They just said, "Poor Emily. Her kinsfolk should come to her." She had some kin in Alabama; but years ago her father had fallen out with them over the estate of old lady Wyatt, the crazy woman, and there was no communication between the two families. They had not even been represented at the funeral.

And as soon as the old people said, "Poor Emily," the whispering began. "Do you suppose it's really so?" they said to one another. "Of course it is. What else could . . ." This behind their hands; rustling of craned silk and satin behind jalousies closed upon the sun of Sunday afternoon as the thin, swift clop-clop-clop of the matched team passed: "Poor Emily."

She carried her head high enough—even when we believed that she was fallen. It was as if she demanded more than ever the recognition of her dignity as the last Grierson; as if it had wanted that touch of earthiness to reaffirm her imperviousness. Like when she bought the rat poison, the arsenic. That was over a year after they had begun to say "Poor Emily," and while the two female cousins were visiting her.

"I want some poison," she said to the druggist. She was over thirty then, still a slight woman, though thinner than usual, with cold, haughty black eyes in a face the flesh of which was strained across the temples and about the eye-sockets as you imagine a lighthouse-keeper's face ought to look. "I want some poison," she said.

"Yes, Miss Emily. What kind? For rats and such? I'd recom—"

"I want the best you have. I don't care what kind."

The druggist named several. "They'll kill anything up to an elephant. But what you want is—"

"Arsenic," Miss Emily said. "Is that a good one?"

"Is . . . arsenic? Yes, ma'am. But what you want—"

"I want arsenic."

The druggist looked down at her. She looked back at him, erect, her face like a strained flag. "Why, of course," the druggist said. "If that's what you want. But the law requires you to tell what you are going to use it for."

Miss Emily just stared at him, her head tilted back in order to look him eye for eye, until he looked away and went and got the arsenic and wrapped it up. The Negro delivery boy brought her the package; the druggist didn't come back. When she opened the package at home there was written on the box, under the skull and bones: "For rats."

IV

SO the next day we all said, "She will kill herself"; and we said it would be the best thing. When she had first begun to be seen with Homer Barron, we had said, "She will marry him." Then we said, "She will persuade him yet," because Homer himself had remarked—he liked men, and it as known that he drank with the younger men in the Elks' Club—that he was not a marrying man. Later we said, "Poor Emily" behind the jalousies as they passed on Sunday afternoon in the glittering buggy,

Miss Emily with her head high and Homer Barron with his hat cocked and a cigar in his teeth, reins and whip in a yellow glove.

Then some of the ladies began to say that it was a disgrace to the town and a bad example to the young people. The men did not want to interfere, but at last the ladies forced the Baptist minister—Miss Emily's people were Episcopal—to call upon her. He would never divulge what happened during that interview, but he refused to go back again. The next Sunday they again drove about the streets, and the following day the minister's wife wrote to Miss Emily's relations in Alabama.

So she had blood-kin under her roof again and we sat back to watch developments. At first nothing happened. Then we were sure that they were to be married. We learned that Miss Emily had been to the jeweler's and ordered a man's toilet set in silver, with the letters H. B. on each piece. Two days later we learned that she had bought a complete outfit of men's clothing, including a nightshirt, and we said, "They are married." We were really glad. We were glad because the two female cousins were even more Grierson than Miss Emily had ever been.

So we were not surprised when Homer Barron—the streets had been finished some time since—was gone. We were a little disappointed that there was not a public blowing-off, but we believed that he had gone on to prepare for Miss Emily's coming, or to give her a chance to get rid of the cousins. (By that time it was a cabal, and we were all Miss Emily's allies to help circumvent the cousins.) Sure enough, after another week they departed. And, as we had expected all along, within three days Homer Barron was back in town. A neighbor saw the Negro man admit him at the kitchen door at dusk one evening.

And that was the last we saw of Homer Barron. And of Miss Emily for some time. The Negro man went in and out with the market basket, but the front door remained closed. Now and then we would see her at a window for a moment, as the men did that night when they sprinkled the lime, but for almost six months she did not appear on the streets. Then we knew that this was to be expected too; as if that quality of her father which had thwarted her woman's life so many times had been too virulent and too furious to die.

When we next saw Miss Emily, she had grown fat and her hair was turning gray. During the next few years it grew grayer and grayer until it attained an even pepper-and-salt iron-gray, when it ceased turning. Up to the day of her death at seventy-four it was still that vigorous iron-gray, like the hair of an active man.

From that time on her front door remained closed, save for a period of six or seven years, when she was about forty, during which she gave lessons in china-painting. She fitted up a studio in one of the downstairs rooms, where the daughters and granddaughters of Colonel Sartoris' contemporaries were sent to her with the same regularity and in the same spirit that they were sent to church on Sundays with a twenty-five-cent piece for the collection plate. Meanwhile her taxes had been remitted.

Then the newer generation became the backbone and the spirit of the town, and the painting pupils grew up and fell away and did not send their children to her with boxes of color and tedious brushes and pictures cut from the ladies' magazines. The front door closed upon the last one and remained closed for good. When the town got free postal delivery, Miss Emily alone refused to let them fasten the metal numbers above her door and attach a mailbox to it. She would not listen to them.

Daily, monthly, yearly we watched the Negro grow grayer and more stooped, going in and out with the market basket. Each December we sent her a tax notice, which would be returned by the post office a week later, unclaimed. Now and then we would see her in one of the downstairs windows—she had evidently shut up the top floor of the house—like the carven torso of an idol in a niche, looking or not looking at us, we could never tell which. Thus she passed from generation to generation—dear, inescapable, impervious, tranquil, and perverse.

And so she died. Fell ill in the house filled with dust and shadows, with only a doddering Negro man to wait on her. We did not even know she was sick; we had long since given up trying to get any information from the Negro. He talked to no one, probably not even to her, for his voice had grown harsh and rusty, as if from disuse.

She died in one of the downstairs rooms, in a heavy walnut bed with a curtain, her gray head propped on a pillow yellow and moldy with age and lack of sunlight.

V

THE Negro met the first of the ladies at the front door and let them in, with their hushed, sibilant voices and their quick, curious glances, and then he disappeared. He walked right through the house and out the back and was not seen again.

The two female cousins came at once. They held the funeral on the second day, with the town coming to look at Miss Emily beneath a mass of bought flowers, with the crayon face of her father musing profoundly above the bier and the ladies sibilant and macabre; and the very old men—some in their brushed Confederate uniforms—on the porch and the lawn, talking of Miss Emily as if she had been a contemporary of theirs, believing that they had danced with her and courted her perhaps, confusing time with its mathematical progression, as the old do, to whom all the past is not a diminishing road but, instead, a huge meadow which no winter ever quite touches, divided from them now by the narrow bottle-neck of the most recent decade of years.

Already we knew that there was one room in that region above stairs which no one had seen in forty years, and which would have to be forced. They waited until Miss Emily was decently in the ground before they opened it.

The violence of breaking down the door seemed to fill this room with pervading dust. A thin, acrid pall as of the tomb seemed to lie everywhere upon this room decked and furnished as for a bridal: upon the valance curtains of faded rose color, upon the rose-shaded lights, upon the dressing table, upon the delicate array of crystal and the man's toilet things backed with tarnished silver, silver so tarnished that the monogram was obscured. Among them lay a collar and tie, as if they had just been removed, which, lifted, left upon the surface a pale crescent in the dust. Upon a chair hung the suit, carefully folded; beneath it the two mute shoes and the discarded socks.

The man himself lay in the bed.

For a long while we just stood there, looking down at the profound and fleshless grin. The body had apparently once lain in the attitude of an embrace, but now the long sleep that outlast love, that conquers even the grimace of love, had cuckolded him. What was left of him, rotted beneath what was left of the nightshirt, had become inextricable from the bed in which he lay; and upon him and upon the pillow beside him lay that even coating of the patient and biding dust.

Then we noticed that in the second pillow was the indentation of a head. One of us lifted something from it, and leaning forward, that faint and invisible dust dry and acrid in the nostrils, we saw a long strand of iron-gray hair.

Spotted Horses

William Faulkner

I

YES, sir. Flem Snopes has filled that whole country full of
spotted horses. You can hear folks running them all day and
all night, whooping and hollering, and the horses running
back and forth across them little wooden bridges ever now
and then kind of like thunder. Here I was this morning pretty
near half way to town, with the team ambling along and me
setting in the buckboard about half asleep, when all of a sudden something come swurging up outen the bushes and
jumped the road clean, without touching hoof to it. It flew
right over my team, big as a billboard and flying through the
air like a hawk. It taken me thirty minutes to stop my team
and untangle the harness and the buckboard and hitch them
up again.

That Flem Snopes. I be dog if he ain't a case, now. One
morning about ten years ago, the boys was just getting settled
down on Varner's porch for a little talk and tobacco, when here
come Flem out from behind the counter, with his coat off and
his hair all parted, like he might have been clerking for Varner
for ten years already. Folks all knowed him; it was a big family
of them about five miles down the bottom. That year, at least.
Share-cropping. They never stayed on any place over a year.
Then they would move on to another place, with the chap or
maybe the twins of that year's litter. It was a regular nest of
them. But Flem. The rest of them stayed tenant farmers, moving every year, but here come Flem one day, walking out from
behind Jody Varner's counter like he owned it. And he wasn't
there but a year or two before folks knowed that, if him and
Jody was both still in that store in ten years more, it would be
Jody clerking for Flem Snopes. Why, that fellow could make a
nickel where it wasn't but four cents to begin with. He skun me
in two trades, myself, and the fellow that can do that, I just
hope he'll get rich before I do; that's all.

All right. So here Flem was, clerking at Varner's, making a nickel here and there and not telling nobody about it. No, sir. Folks never knowed when Flem got the better of somebody lessen the fellow he beat told it. He'd just set there in the store-chair, chewing his tobacco and keeping his own business to hisself, until about a week later we'd find out it was somebody else's business he was keeping to hisself—provided the fellow he trimmed was mad enough to tell it. That's Flem.

We give him ten years to own ever thing Jody Varner had. But he never waited no ten years. I reckon you-all know that gal of Uncle Billy Varner's, the youngest one; Eula. Jody's sister. Ever Sunday ever yellow-wheeled buggy and curried riding horse in that country would be hitched to Bill Varner's fence, and the young bucks setting on the porch, swarming around Eula like bees around a honey pot. One of these here kind of big, soft-looking gals that could giggle richer than plowed new-ground. Wouldn't none of them leave before the others, and so they would set there on the porch until time to go home, with some of them with nine and ten miles to ride and then get up tomor-row and go back to the field. So they would all leave together and they would ride in a clump down to the creek ford and hitch them curried horses and yellow-wheeled buggies and get out and fight one another. Then they would get in the buggies again and go on home.

Well, one day about a year ago, one of them yellow-wheeled buggies and one of them curried saddle-horses quit this coun-try. We heard they was heading for Texas. The next day Uncle Billy and Eula and Flem come in to town in Uncle Bill's surrey, and when they come back, Flem and Eula was married. And on the next day we heard that two more of them yellow-wheeled buggies had left the country. They mought have gone to Texas, too. It's a big place.

Anyway, about a month after the wedding, Flem and Eula went to Texas, too. They was gone pretty near a year. Then one day last month, Eula come back, with a baby. We figgured up, and we decided that it was as well-growed a three-months-old baby as we ever see. It can already pull up on a chair. I reckon Texas makes big men quick, being a big place. Anyway, if it keeps on like it started, it'll be chewing tobacco and voting time it's eight years old.

And so last Friday here come Flem himself. He was on a wagon with another fellow. The other fellow had one of these two-gallon hats and a ivory-handled pistol and a box of gingersnaps sticking out of his hind pocket, and tied to the tailgate of the wagon was about two dozen of them Texas ponies, hitched to one another with barbed wire. They was colored like parrots and they was quiet as doves, and ere a one of them would kill you quick as a rattlesnake. Nere a one of them had two eyes the same color, and nere a one of them had ever see a bridle, I reckon; and when that Texas man got down offen the wagon and walked up to them to show how gentle they was, one of them cut his vest clean offen him, same as with a razor.

Flem had done already disappeared; he had went on to see his wife, I reckon, and to see if that ere baby had done gone on to the field to help Uncle Billy plow maybe. It was the Texas man that taken the horses on to Mrs. Littlejohn's lot. He had a little trouble at first, when they come to the gate, because they hadn't never see a fence before, and when he finally got them in and taken a pair of wire cutters and unhitched them and got them into the barn and poured some shell corn into the trough, they durn nigh tore down the barn. I reckon they thought that shell corn was bugs, maybe. So he left them in the lot and he announced that the auction would begin at sunup to-morrow.

That night we was setting on Mrs. Littlejohn's porch. You-all mind the moon was nigh full that night, and we could watch them spotted varmints swirling along the fence and back and forth across the lot same as minnows in a pond. And then now and then they would all kind of huddle up against the barn and rest themselves by biting and kicking one another. We would hear a squeal, and then a set of hoofs would go Bam! against the barn, like a pistol. It sounded just like a fellow with a pistol, in a nest of cattymounts, taking his time.

II

IT wasn't ere a man knowed yet if Flem owned them things or not. They just knowed one thing: that they wasn't never going to know for sho if Flem did or not, or if maybe he didn't just get on that wagon at the edge of town, for the ride or not. Even Eck Snopes didn't know, Flem's own cousin. But wasn't nobody surprised at that. We knowed that Flem would skin Eck quick as he would ere a one of us.

They was there by sunup next morning, some of them come twelve and sixteen miles, with seed-money tied up in tobacco sacks in their overalls, standing along the fence, when the Texas man come out of Mrs. Littlejohn's after breakfast and clumb onto the gate post with that ere white pistol butt sticking outen his hind pocket. He taken a new box of gingersnaps outen his pocket and bit the end offen it like a cigar and spit out the paper, and said the auction was open. And still they was coming up in wagons and a horse- and mule-back and hitching the teams across the road and coming to the fence. Flem wasn't nowhere in sight.

But he couldn't get them started. He begun to work on Eck, because Eck holp him last night to get them into the barn and feed them that shell corn. Eck got out just in time. He come outen that barn like a chip on the crest of a busted dam of water, and clumb into the wagon just in time.

He was working on Eck when Henry Armstid come up in his wagon. Eck was saying he was skeered to bid on one of them, because he might get it, and the Texas man says, "Them ponies? Them little horses?" He clumb down offen the gate post and went toward the horses. They broke and run, and him following them, kind of chirping to them, with his hand out like he was fixing to catch a fly, until he got three or four of them cornered. Then he jumped into them, and then we couldn't see nothing for a while because of the dust. It was a big cloud of it, and them blare-eyed, spotted things swoaring outen it twenty foot to a jump, in forty directions without counting up. Then the dust settled and there they was, that Texas man and the horse. He had its head twisted clean around like a owl's head. Its legs was braced and it was trembling like a new bride and groaning like a saw mill, and him holding its head wrung clean around on its neck so it was snuffing sky. "Look it over," he says, with his heels dug too and that white pistol sticking outen his pocket and his neck swole up like a spreading adder's until you could just tell what he was saying, cussing the horse and talking to us all at once: "Look him over, the fiddleheaded son of fourteen fathers. Try him, buy him; you will get the best—" Then it was all dust again, and we couldn't see nothing but spotted hide and mane, and that ere Texas man's bootheels like a couple of walnuts on two strings, and after a while that two-gallon hat come sailing out like a fat old hen crossing a fence.

When the dust settled again, he was just getting outen the far fence corner, brushing himself off. He come and got his hat and brushed it off and come and clumb onto the gate post again. He was breathing hard. He taken the gingersnap box outen his pocket and et one, breathing hard. The hammerhead horse was still running round and round the lot like a merry-go-round at a fair. That was when Henry Armstid come shoving up to the gate in them patched overalls and one of them dangle-armed shirts of hisn. Hadn't nobody noticed him until then. We was all watching the Texas man and the horses. Even Mrs. Littlejohn; she had done come out and built a fire under the wash-pot in her back yard, and she would stand at the fence a while and then go back into the house and come out again with a arm full of wash and stand at the fence again. Well, here come Henry shoving up, and then we see Mrs. Armstid right behind him, in that ere faded wrapper and sunbonnet and them tennis shoes. "Git on back to that wagon," Henry says.

"Henry," she says.

"Here, boys," the Texas man says; "make room for missus to git up and see. Come on, Henry," he says; "here's your chance to buy that saddle-horse missus has been wanting. What about ten dollars, Henry?"

"Henry," Mrs. Armstid says. She put her hand on Henry's arm. Henry knocked her hand down.

"Git on back to that wagon, like I told you," he says.

Mrs. Armstid never moved. She stood behind Henry, with her hands rolled into her dress, not looking at nothing. "He hain't no more despair than to buy one of them things," she says. "And us not five dollars ahead of the pore house, he hain't no more despair." It was the truth, too. They ain't never made more than a bare living offen that place of theirs, and them with four chaps and the very clothes they wears she earns by weaving by the firelight at night while Henry's asleep.

"Shut your mouth and git on back to that wagon," Henry says. "Do you want I take a wagon stake to you here in the big road?"

Well, that Texas man taken one look at her. Then he begun on Eck again, like Henry wasn't even there. But Eck was skeered. "I can git me a snapping turtle or a water moccasin for nothing. I ain't going to buy none."

So the Texas man said he would give Eck a horse. "To start the auction, and because you holp me last night. If you'll start the bidding on the next horse," he says, "I'll give you that fiddlehead horse."

I wish you could have seen them, standing there with their seed-money in their pockets, watching that Texas man give Eck Snopes a live horse, all fixed to call him a fool if he taken it or not. Finally Eck says he'll take it. "Only I just starts the bidding," he says. "I don't have to buy the next one lessen I ain't overtopped." The Texas man said all right, and Eck bid a dollar on the next one, with Henry Armstid standing there with his mouth already open, watching Eck and the Texas man like a mad-dog or something. "A dollar," Eck says.

The Texas man looked at Eck. His mouth was already open too, like he had started to say something and what he was going to say had up and died on him. "A dollar?" he says. "One dollar? You mean, *one* dollar, Eck?"

"Durn it," Eck says; "two dollars, then."

Well, sir, I wish you could a seen that Texas man. He taken out that gingersnap box and held it up and looked into it, careful, like it might have been a diamond ring in it, or a spider. Then he throwed it away and wiped his face with a bandanna. "Well," he says. "Well. Two dollars. Two dollars. Is your pulse all right, Eck?" he says. "Do you have ager-sweats at night, maybe?" he says. "Well," he says, "I got to take it. But are you boys going to stand there and see Eck get two horses at a dollar a head?"

That done it. I be dog if he wasn't nigh as smart as Flem Snopes. He hadn't no more than got the words outen his mouth before here was Henry Armstid, waving his hand. "Three dollars," Henry says. Mrs. Armstid tried to hold him again. He knocked her hand off, shoving up to the gate post.

"Mister," Mrs. Armstid says, "we got chaps in the house and not corn to feed the stock. We got five dollars I earned my chaps a-weaving after dark, and him snoring in the bed. And he hain't no more despair."

"Henry bids three dollars," the Texas man says. "Raise him a dollar, Eck, and the horse is yours."

"Henry," Mrs. Armstid says.

"Raise him, Eck," the Texas man says.

"Four dollars," Eck says.

"Five dollars," Henry says, shaking his fist. He shoved up

right under the gate post. Mrs. Armstid was looking at the Texas man too.

"Mister," she says, "if you take that five dollars I earned my chaps a-weaving for one of them things, it'll be a curse onto you and yourn during all the time of man."

But it wasn't no stopping Henry. He had shoved up, waving his fist at the Texas man. He opened it; the money was in nickels and quarters, and one dollar bill that looked like a cow's cud. "Five dollars," he says. "And the man that raises it'll have to beat my head off, or I'll beat hisn."

"All right," the Texas man says. "Five dollars is bid. But don't you shake your hand at me."

III

IT taken till nigh sundown before the last one was sold. He got them hotted up once and the bidding got up to seven dollars and a quarter, but most of them went around three or four dollars, him setting on the gate post and picking the horses out one at a time by mouth-word, and Mrs. Littlejohn pumping up and down at the tub and stopping and coming to the fence for a while and going back to the tub again. She had done got done too, and the wash was hung on the line in the back yard, and we could smell supper cooking. Finally they was all sold; he swapped the last two and the wagon for a buckboard.

We was all kind of tired, but Henry Armstid looked more like a mad-dog than ever. When he bought, Mrs. Armstid had went back to the wagon, setting in it behind them two rabbit-sized, bone-pore mules, and the wagon itself looking like it would fall all to pieces soon as the mules moved. Henry hadn't even waited to pull it outen the road; it was still in the middle of the road and her setting in it, not looking at nothing, ever since this morning.

Henry was right up against the gate. He went up to the Texas man. "I bought a horse and I paid cash," Henry says. "And yet you expect me to stand around here until they are all sold before I can get my horse. I'm going to take my horse outen that lot."

The Texas man looked at Henry. He talked like he might have been asking for a cup of coffee at the table. "Take your horse," he says.

Then Henry quit looking at the Texas man. He begun to swallow, holding onto the gate. "Ain't you going to help me?" he says.

"It ain't my horse," the Texas man says.

Henry never looked at the Texas man again, he never looked at nobody. "Who'll help me catch my horse?" he says. Never nobody said nothing. "Bring the plowline," Henry says. Mrs. Armstid got outen the wagon and brought the plowline. The Texas man got down offen the post. The woman made to pass him, carrying the rope.

"Don't you go in there, missus," the Texas man says.

Henry opened the gate. He didn't look back. "Come on here," he says.

Mrs. Armstid wasn't looking at nobody, neither, with her hands across her middle, holding the rope. "I reckon I better," she says. Her and Henry went into the lot. The horses broke and run. Henry and Mrs. Armstid followed.

"Get him into the corner," Henry says. They got Henry's horse cornered finally, and Henry taken the rope, but Mrs. Armstid let the horse get out. They hemmed it up again, but Mrs. Armstid let it get out again, and Henry turned and hit her with the rope. "Why didn't you head him back?" Henry says. He hit her again. "Why didn't you?" It was about that time I looked around and see Flem Snopes standing there.

It was the Texas man that done something. He moved fast for a big man. He caught the rope before Henry could hit the third time, and Henry whirled and made like he would jump at the Texas man. But he never jumped. The Texas man went and taken Henry's arm and led him outen the lot. Mrs. Armstid come behind them and the Texas man taken some money outen his pocket and he give it into Mrs. Armstid's hand. "Get him into the wagon and take him on home," the Texas man says, like he might have been telling them he enjoyed his supper.

Then here come Flem. "What's that for, Buck?" Flem says.

"Thinks he bought one of them ponies," the Texas man says. "Get him on away, missus."

But Henry wouldn't go. "Give him back that money," he says. "I bought that horse and I aim to have him if I have to shoot him."

And there was Flem, standing there with his hands in his pockets, chewing, like he had just happened to be passing.

"You take your money and I take my horse," Henry says. "Give it back to him," he says to Mrs. Armstid.

"You don't own no horse of mine," the Texas man says. "Get him on home, missus."

Then Henry seen Flem. "You got something to do with these horses," he says. "I bought one. Here's the money for it." He taken the bill outen Mrs. Armstid's hand. He offered it to Flem. "I bought one. Ask him. Here's the money," he says, giving the bill to Flem.

When Flem taken the money, the Texas man dropped the rope he had snatched outen Henry's hand. He had done sent Eck Snopes's boy up to the store for another box of gingersnaps, and he taken the box outen his pocket and looked into it. It was empty and he dropped it on the ground. "Mr. Snopes will have your money for you to-morrow," he says to Mrs. Armstid. "You can get it from him to-morrow. He don't own no horse. You get him into the wagon and get him on home." Mrs. Armstid went back to the wagon and got in. "Where's that ere buckboard I bought?" the Texas man says. It was after sundown then. And then Mrs. Little-john come out on the porch and rung the supper bell.

IV

I come on in and et supper. Mrs. Littlejohn would bring in a pan of bread or something, then she would go out to the porch a minute and come back and tell us. The Texas man had hitched his team to the buckboard he had swapped them last two horses for, and him and Flem had gone, and then she told that the rest of them that never had ropes had went back to the store with I. O. Snopes to get some ropes, and wasn't nobody at the gate but Henry Armstid, and Mrs. Armstid setting in the wagon in the road, and Eck Snopes and that boy of hisn. "I don't care how many of them fool men gets killed by them things," Mrs. Littlejohn says, "but I ain't going to let Eck Snopes take that boy into that lot again." So she went down to the gate, but she come back without the boy or Eck neither.

"It ain't no need to worry about that boy," I says. "He's charmed." He was right behind Eck last night when Eck went to help feed them. The whole drove of them jumped clean over that boy's head and never touched him. It was Eck that touched him. Eck snatched him into the wagon and taken a rope and frailed the tar outen him.

So I had done et and went to my room and was undressing, long as I had a long trip to make next day; I was trying to sell a machine to Mrs. Bundren up past Whiteleaf; when Henry Armstid opened that gate and went in by hisself. They couldn't make him wait for the balance of them to get back with their ropes. Eck Snopes said he tried to make Henry wait, but Henry wouldn't do it. Eck said Henry walked right up to them and that when they broke, they run clean over Henry like a haymow breaking down. Eck said he snatched that boy of hisn out of the way just in time and that them things went through that gate like a creek flood and into the wagons and teams hitched side the road, busting wagon tongues and snapping harness like it was fishing-line, with Mrs. Armstid still setting in their wagon in the middle of it like something carved outen wood. Then they scattered, wild horses and tame mules with pieces of harness and single trees dangling offen them, both ways up and down the road.

"There goes ourn, paw!" Eck says his boy said. "There it goes, into Mrs. Littlejohn's house." Eck says it run right up the steps and into the house like a boarder late for supper. I reckon so. Anyway, I was in my room, in my underclothes, with one sock on and one sock in my hand, leaning out the window when the commotion busted out, when I heard something run into the melodeon in the hall; it sounded like a railroad engine. Then the door to my room come sailing in like when you throw a tin bucket top into the wind and I looked over my shoulder and see something that looked like a fourteen-foot pinwheel a-blaring its eyes at me. It had to blare them fast, because I was already done jumped out the window.

I reckon it was anxious, too. I reckon it hadn't never seen barbed wire or shell corn before, but I know it hadn't never seen underclothes before, or maybe it was a sewing-machine agent it hadn't never seen. Anyway, it swirled and turned to run back up the hall and outen the house, when it met Eck Snopes and that boy just coming in, carrying a rope. It swirled again and run down the hall and out the back door just in time to meet Mrs. Littlejohn. She had just gathered up the clothes she had washed, and she was coming onto the back porch with a armful of washing in one hand and a scrubbing-board in the other, when the horse skidded up to her, trying to stop and swirl again. It never taken Mrs. Littlejohn no time a-tall.

"Git outen here, you son," she says. She hit it across the face with the scrubbing-board; that ere scrubbing-board split as neat as ere a axe could have done it, and when the horse swirled to run back up the hall, she hit it again with what was left of the scrubbing-board, not on the head this time. "And stay out," she says.

Eck and that boy was half-way down the hall by this time. I reckon that horse looked like a pinwheel to Eck too. "Git to hell outen here, Ad!" Eck says. Only there wasn't time. Eck dropped flat on his face, but the boy never moved. The boy was about a yard tall maybe, in overhalls just like Eck's; that horse swoared over his head without touching a hair. I saw that, because I was just coming back up the front steps, still carrying that ere sock and still in my underclothes, when the horse come onto the porch again. It taken one look at me and swirled again and run to the end of the porch and jumped the banisters and the lot fence like a hen-hawk and lit in the lot running and went out the gate again and jumped eight or ten upside-down wagons and went on down the road. It was a full moon then. Mrs. Armstid was still setting in the wagon like she had done been carved outen wood and left there and forgot.

That horse. It ain't never missed a lick. It was going about forty miles a hour when it come to the bridge over the creek. It would have had a clear road, but it so happened that Vernon Tull was already using the bridge when it got there. He was coming back from town; he hadn't heard about the auction; him and his wife and three daughters and Mrs. Tull's aunt, all setting in chairs in the wagon bed, and all asleep, including the mules. They waked up when the horse hit the bridge one time, but Tull said the first he knew was when the mules tried to turn the wagon around in the middle of the bridge and he seen that spotted varmint run right twixt the mules and run up the wagon tongue like a squirrel. He said he just had time to hit it across the face with his whip-stock, because about that time the mules turned the wagon around on that ere one-way bridge and that horse clumb across one of the mules and jumped down onto the bridge again and went on, with Vernon standing up in the wagon and kicking at it.

Tull said the mules turned in the harness and clumb back into the wagon too, with Tull trying to beat them out again, with the reins wrapped around his wrist. After that he says all he

seen was overturned chairs and womenfolks' legs and white
drawers shining in the moonlight, and his mules and that spotted horse going on up the road like a ghost.

The mules jerked Tull outen the wagon and drug him a spell
on the bridge before the reins broke. They thought at first that
he was dead, and while they was kneeling around him, picking
the bridge splinters outen him, here come Eck and that boy,
still carrying the rope. They was running and breathing a little
hard. "Where'd he go?" Eck says.

V

I went back and got my pants and shirt and shoes on just in
time to go and help get Henry Armstid outen the trash in the
lot. I be dog if he didn't look like he was dead, with his head
hanging back and his teeth showing in the moonlight, and a little rim of white under his eyelids. We could still hear them
horses, here and there; hadn't none of them got more than four-
five miles away yet, not knowing the country, I reckon. So we
could hear them and folks yelling now and then: "Whooey. Head
him!"

We toted Henry into Mrs. Littlejohn's. She was in the hall; she
hadn't put down the armful of clothes. She taken one look at
us, and she laid down the busted scrubbing-board and taken
up the lamp and opened a empty door. "Bring him in here," she
says.

We toted him in and laid him on the bed. Mrs. Littlejohn set
the lamp on the dresser, still carrying the clothes. "I'll declare,
you men," she says. Our shadows was way up the wall, tiptoe-
ing too; we could hear ourselves breathing. "Better get his wife,"
Mrs. Littlejohn says. She went out, carrying the clothes.

"I reckon we had," Quick says. "Go get her, somebody."

"Whyn't you go?" Winterbottom says.

"Let Ernest git her," Durley says. "He lives neighbors with
them."

Ernest went to fetch her. I be dog if Henry didn't look like he
was dead. Mrs. Littlejohn come back, with a kettle and some
towels. She went to work on Henry, and then Mrs. Armstid and
Ernest come in. Mrs. Armstid come to the foot of the bed and
stood there, with her hands rolled into her apron, watching
what Mrs. Littlejohn was doing, I reckon.

"You men git outen the way," Mrs. Littlejohn says. "Git outside," she says. "See if you can't find something else to play with that will kill some more of you."

"Is he dead?" Winterbottom says.

"It ain't your fault if he ain't," Mrs. Littlejohn says. "Go tell Will Varner to come up here. I reckon a man ain't so different from a mule, come long come short. Except maybe a mule's got more sense."

We went to get Uncle Billy. It was a full moon. We could hear them, now and then, four mile away: "Whooey. Head him." The country was full of them, one on ever wooden bridge in the land, running across it like thunder: "Whooey. There he goes. Head him."

We hadn't got far before Henry begun to scream. I reckon Mrs. Littlejohn's water had brung him to; anyway, he wasn't dead. We went on to Uncle Billy's. The house was dark. We called to him, and after a while the window opened and Uncle Billy put his head out, peart as a peckerwood, listening. "Are they still trying to catch them durn rabbits?" he says.

He come down, with his britches on over his night-shirt and his suspenders dangling, carrying his horse-doctoring grip. "Yes, sir," he says, cocking his head like a woodpecker; "they're still a-trying."

We could hear Henry before we reached Mrs. Littlejohn's. He was going Ah-Ah-Ah. We stopped in the yard. Uncle Billy went on in. We could hear Henry. We stood in the yard, hearing them on the bridges, this-a-way and that: "Whooey. Whooey."

"Eck Snopes ought to caught hisn," Ernest says.

"Looks like he ought," Winterbottom said.

Henry was going Ah-Ah-Ah steady in the house; then he begun to scream. "Uncle Billy's started," Quick says. We looked into the hall. We could see the light where the door was. Then Mrs. Littlejohn come out.

"Will needs some help," she says. "You, Ernest. You'll do." Ernest went into the house.

"Hear them?" Quick said. "That one was on Four Mile bridge." We could hear them; it sounded like thunder a long way off; it didn't last long:

"Whooey."

We could hear Henry: "Ah-Ah-Ah-Ah-Ah."

"They are both started now," Winterbottom says. "Ernest too."

That was early in the night. Which was a good thing, because it taken a long night for folks to chase them things right and for Henry to lay there and holler, being as Uncle Billy never had none of this here chloryfoam to set Henry's leg with. So it was considerate in Flem to get them started early. And what do you reckon Flem's com-ment was?

That's right. Nothing. Because he wasn't there. Hadn't nobody see him since that Texas man left.

VI

THAT was Saturday night. I reckon Mrs. Armstid got home about daylight, to see about the chaps. I don't know where they thought her and Henry was. But lucky the oldest one was a gal, about twelve, big enough to take care of the little ones. Which she did for the next two days. Mrs. Armstid would nurse Henry all night and work in the kitchen for hern and Henry's keep, and in the afternoon she would drive home (it was about four miles) to see to the chaps. She would cook up a pot of victuals and leave it on the stove, and the gal would bar the house and keep the little ones quiet. I would hear Mrs. Littlejohn and Mrs. Armstid talking in the kitchen. "How are the chaps making out?" Mrs. Littlejohn says.

"All right," Mrs. Armstid says.

"Don't they git skeered at night?" Mrs. Littlejohn says.

"Ina May bars the door when I leave," Mrs. Armstid says. "She's got the axe in bed with her. I reckon she can make out."

I reckon they did. And I reckon Mrs. Armstid was waiting for Flem to come back to town; hadn't nobody seen him until this morning; to get her money the Texas man said Flem was keeping for her. Sho. I reckon she was.

Anyway, I heard Mrs. Armstid and Mrs. Littlejohn talking in the kitchen this morning while I was eating breakfast. Mrs. Littlejohn had just told Mrs. Armstid that Flem was in town. "You can ask him for that five dollars," Mrs. Littlejohn says.

"You reckon he'll give it to me?" Mrs. Armstid says.

Mrs. Littlejohn was washing dishes, washing them like a man, like they was made out of iron. "No," she says. "But asking him won't do no hurt. It might shame him. I don't reckon it will, but it might."

"If he wouldn't give it back, it ain't no use to ask," Mrs. Armstid says.

"Suit yourself," Mrs. Littlejohn says. "It's your money."

I could hear the dishes.

"Do you reckon he might give it back to me?" Mrs. Armstid says. "That Texas man said he would. He said I could get it from Mr. Snopes later."

"Then go and ask him for it," Mrs. Littlejohn says.

I could hear the dishes.

"He won't give it back to me," Mrs. Armstid says.

"All right," Mrs. Littlejohn says. "Don't ask him for it, then."

I could hear the dishes; Mrs. Armstid was helping. "You don't reckon he would, do you?" she says. Mrs. Littlejohn never said nothing. It sounded like she was throwing the dishes at one another. "Maybe I better go and talk to Henry about it," Mrs. Armstid says.

"I would," Mrs. Littlejohn says. I be dog if it didn't sound like she had two plates in her hands, beating them together. "Then Henry can buy another five-dollar horse with it. Maybe he'll buy one next time that will out and out kill him. If I thought that, I'd give you back the money, myself."

"I reckon I better talk to him first," Mrs. Armstid said. Then it sounded like Mrs. Littlejohn taken up all the dishes and throwed them at the cook-stove, and I come away.

That was this morning. I had been up to Bundren's and back, and I thought that things would have kind of settled down. So after breakfast, I went up to the store. And there was Flem, setting in the store-chair and whittling, like he might not have ever moved since he come to clerk for Jody Varner. I. O. was leaning in the door, in his shirt sleeves and with his hair parted too, same as Flem was before he turned the clerking job over to I. O. It's a funny thing about them Snopes: they all looks alike, yet there ain't ere a two of them that claims brothers. They're always just cousins, like Flem and Eck and Flem and I. O. Eck was there too, squatting against the wall, him and that boy, eating cheese and crackers outen a sack; they told me that Eck hadn't been home a-tall. And that Lon Quick hadn't got back to town, even. He followed his horse clean down to Samson's Bridge, with a wagon and a camp outfit. Eck finally caught one of hisn. It run into a blind lane at Freeman's and Eck and the boy taken and tied their rope across the end of the lane, about three foot high. The horse come to the end of the lane and whirled and run back without ever stopping. Eck says it never seen the rope a-tall. He says it looked just like one of these here Christmas pinwheels. "Didn't it try to run again?" I says.

"No," Eck says, eating a bite of cheese offen his knife blade. "Just kicked some."

"Kicked some?" I says.

"It broke its neck," Eck says.

Well, they was squatting there, about six of them, talking, talking at Flem; never nobody knowed yet if Flem had ere a interest in them horses or not. So finally I come right out and asked him. "Flem's done skun all of us so much," I says, "that we're proud of him. Come on, Flem," I says, "how much did you and that Texas man make offen them horses? You can tell us. Ain't nobody here but Eck that bought one of them; the others ain't got back to town yet, and Eck's your own cousin; he'll be proud to hear, too. How much did you-all make?"

They was all whittling, not looking at Flem, making like they was studying. But you could a heard a pin drop. And I. O. He had been rubbing his back up and down on the door, but he stopped now, watching Flem like a pointing dog. Flem finished cutting the sliver offen his stick. He spit across the porch, into the road. "'Twarn't none of my horses," he says.

I. O. cackled, like a hen, slapping his legs with both hands. "You boys might just as well quit trying to get ahead of Flem," he said.

Well, about that time I see Mrs. Armstid come outen Mrs. Littlejohn's gate, coming up the road. I never said nothing. I says, "Well, if a man can't take care of himself in a trade, he can't blame the man that trims him."

Flem never said nothing, trimming at the stick. He hadn't seen Mrs. Armstid. "Yes, sir," I says. "A fellow like Henry Armstid ain't got nobody but hisself to blame."

"Course he ain't," I. O. says. He ain't seen her, neither. "Henry Armstid's a born fool. Always is been. If Flem hadn't a got his money, somebody else would."

We looked at Flem. He never moved. Mrs. Armstid come on up the road.

"That's right," I says. "But, come to think of it, Henry never bought no horse." We looked at Flem; you could a heard a match drop. "That Texas man told her to get that five dollars back from Flem next day. I reckon Flem's done already taken that money to Mrs. Littlejohn's and give it to Mrs. Armstid."

We watched Flem. I. O. quit rubbing his back against the door again. After a while Flem raised his head and spit across the porch, into the dust. I. O. cackled, just like a hen. "Ain't he a beating fellow, now?" I. O. says.

Mrs. Armstid was getting closer, so I kept on talking, watching to see if Flem would look up and see her. But he never looked up. I went on talking about Tull, about how he was going to sue Flem, and Flem setting there, whittling his stick, not saying nothing else after he said they wasn't none of his horses.

Then I. O. happened to look around. He seen Mrs. Armstid. "Psssst!" he says. Flem looked up. "Here she comes!" I. O. says. "Go out the back. I'll tell her you done went in to town to-day."

But Flem never moved. He just set there, whittling, and we watched Mrs. Armstid come up onto the porch, in that ere faded sunbonnet and wrapper and them tennis shoes that made a kind of hissing noise on the porch. She come onto the porch and stopped, her hands rolled into her dress in front, not looking at nothing.

"He said Saturday," she says, "that he wouldn't sell Henry no horse. He said I could get the money from you."

Flem looked up. The knife never stopped. It went on trimming off a sliver same as if he was watching it. "He taken that money off with him when he left," Flem says.

Mrs. Armstid never looked at nothing. We never looked at her, neither, except that boy of Eck's. He had a half-et cracker in his hand, watching her, chewing.

"He said Henry hadn't bought no horse," Mrs. Armstid says. "He said for me to get the money from you today."

"I reckon he forgot about it," Flem said. "He taken that money off with him Saturday." He whittled again. I. O. kept on rubbing his back, slow. He licked his lips. After a while the woman looked up the road, where it went on up the hill, toward the graveyard. She looked up that way for a while, with that boy of Eck's watching her and I. O. rubbing his back slow against the door. Then she turned back toward the steps.

"I reckon it's time to get dinner started," she says.

"How's Henry this morning, Mrs. Armstid?" Winterbottom says.

She looked at Winterbottom; she almost stopped. "He's resting, I thank you kindly," she says.

Flem got up, outen the chair, putting his knife away. He spit across the porch. "Wait a minute, Mrs. Armstid," he says. She stopped again. She didn't look at him. Flem went on into the store, with I. O. done quit rubbing his back now, with his head craned after Flem, and Mrs. Armstid standing there with her hands rolled into her dress, not looking at nothing. A wagon come up the road and passed; it was Freeman, on the way to town. Then Flem come out again, with I. O. still watching him. Flem had one of these little striped sacks of Jody Varner's candy; I bet he still owes Jody that nickel, too. He put the sack into Mrs. Armstid's hand, like he would have put it into a hollow stump. He spit again across the porch. "A little sweetening for the chaps," he says.

"You're right kind," Mrs. Armstid says. She held the sack of candy in her hand, not looking at nothing. Eck's boy was watching the sack, the half-et cracker in his hand; he wasn't chewing now. He watched Mrs. Armstid roll the sack into her apron. "I reckon I better get on back and help with dinner," she says. She turned and went back across the porch. Flem set down in the chair again and opened his knife. He spit across the porch again, past Mrs. Armstid where she hadn't went down the steps yet. Then she went on, in that ere sunbonnet and wrapper all the same color, back down the road toward Mrs. Littlejohn's. You couldn't see her dress move, like a natural woman walking. She looked like a old snag still standing up and moving along on a high water. We watched her turn in at Mrs. Littlejohn's and go outen sight. Flem was whittling. I. O. begun to rub his back on the door. Then he begun to cackle, just like a durn hen.

"You boys might just as well quit trying," I. O. says. "You can't git ahead of Flem. You can't touch him. Ain't he a sight, now?"

I be dog if he ain't. If I had brung a herd of wild cattymounts into town and sold them to my neighbors and kinfolks, they would have lynched me. Yes, sir.

Wunderkind

Carson McCullers

SHE came into the living room, her music satchel plopping against her winter-stockinged legs and her other arm weighted down with schoolbooks, and stood for a moment listening to the sounds from the studio. A soft procession of piano chords and the tuning of a violin. Then Mister Bilderbach called out to her in his chunky, guttural tones:

"That you, Bienchen?"

As she jerked off her mittens she saw that her fingers were twitching to the motions of the fugue she had practiced that morning. "Yes," she answered. "It's me."

"I," the voice corrected. "Just a moment."

She could hear Mister Lafkowitz talking—his words spun out in a silky, unintelligible hum. A voice almost like a woman's, she thought, compared to Mister Bilderbach's. Restlessness scattered her attention. She fumbled with her geometry book and *Le Voyage de Monsieur Perrichon* before putting them on the table. She sat down on the sofa and began to take her music from the satchel. Again she saw her hands—the quivering tendons that stretched down from her knuckles, the sore finger tip cupped with curled, dingy tape. The sight sharpened the fear that had begun to torment her for the past few months.

Noiselessly she mumbled a few phrases of encouragement to herself. A good lesson—a good lesson—like it used to be—Her lips closed as she heard the stolid sound of Mister Bilderbach's footsteps across the floor of the studio and the creaking of the door as it slid open.

For a moment she had the peculiar feeling that during most of the fifteen years of her life she had been looking at the face and shoulders that jutted from behind the door, in a silence disturbed only by the muted, blank plucking of a violin string. Mister Bilderbach. Her teacher, Mister Bilderbach. The quick eyes behind the horn-rimmed glasses; the light, thin hair and the narrow face beneath; the lips full and loose shut and the lower one pink and shining from the bites of his teeth; the forked veins in his temples throbbing plainly enough to be observed across the room.

"Aren't you a little early?" he asked, glancing at the clock on the mantelpiece that had pointed to five minutes of twelve for a month. "Josef's in here. We're running over a little sonatina by someone he knows."

"Good," she said, trying to smile. "I'll listen." She could see her fingers sinking powerless into a blur of piano keys. She felt tired—felt that if he looked at her much longer her hands might tremble.

He stood uncertain, halfway in the room. Sharply his teeth pushed down on his bright, swollen lip. "Hungry, Bienchen?" he asked. "There's some apple cake Anna made, and milk."

"I'll wait till afterward," she said. "Thanks."

"After you finish with a very fine lesson—eh?" His smile seemed to crumble at the corners.

There was a sound from behind him in the studio and Mister Lafkowitz pushed at the other panel of the door and stood beside him.

"Frances?" he said, smiling. "And how is the work coming now?"

Without meaning to, Mister Lafkowitz always made her feel clumsy and overgrown. He was such a small man himself, with a weary look when he was not holding his violin. His eyebrows curved high above his sallow, Jewish face as though asking a question, but the lids of his eyes drowsed languorous and indifferent. Today he seemed distracted. She watched him come into the room for no apparent purpose, holding his pearl-tipped bow in his still fingers, slowly gliding the white horsehair through a chalky piece of rosin. His eyes were sharp bright slits today and the linen handkerchief that flowed down from his collar darkened the shadows beneath them.

"I gather you're doing a lot now," smiled Mister Lafkowitz, although she had not yet answered the question.

She looked at Mister Bilderbach. He turned away. His heavy shoulders pushed the door open wide so that the late afternoon sun came through the window of the studio and shafted yellow over the dusty living room. Behind her teacher she could see the squat long piano, the window, and the bust of Brahms.

"No," she said to Mister Lafkowitz, "I'm doing terribly." Her thin fingers flipped at the pages of her music. "I don't know what's the matter," she said, looking at Mister Bilderbach's stooped muscular back that stood tense and listening.

Mister Lafkowitz smiled. "There are times, I suppose, when one—"

A harsh chord sounded from the piano. "Don't you think we'd better get on with this?" asked Mister Bilderbach.

"Immediately," said Mister Lafkowitz, giving the bow one more scrape before starting toward the door. She could see him pick up his violin from the top of the piano. He caught her eye and lowered the instrument. "You've seen the picture of Heime?"

Her fingers curled tight over the sharp corner of the satchel. "What picture?"

"One of Heime in the *Musical Courier* there on the table. Inside the top cover."

The sonatina began. Discordant yet somehow simple. Empty but with a sharp-cut style of its own. She reached for the magazine and opened it.

There Heime was—in the left-hand corner. Holding his violin with his fingers hooked down over the strings for a pizzicato. With his dark serge knickers strapped neatly beneath his knees, a sweater and rolled collar. It was a bad picture. Although it was snapped in profile his eyes were cut around toward the photographer and his finger looked as though it would pluck the wrong string. He seemed suffering to turn around toward the picture-taking apparatus. He was thinner—his stomach did not poke out now—but he hadn't changed much in six months.

Heime Israelsky, talented young violinist, snapped while at work in his teacher's studio on Riverside Drive. Young Master Israelsky, who will soon celebrate his fifteenth birthday, has been invited to play the Beethoven Concerto with—

That morning, after she had practiced from six until eight, her dad had made her sit down at the table with the family for breakfast. She hated breakfast; it gave her a sick feeling afterward. She would rather wait and get four chocolate bars with her twenty cents lunch money and munch them during school—bringing up little morsels from her pocket under cover of her handkerchief, stopping dead when the silver paper rattled. But this morning her dad had put a fried egg on her plate and she had known that if it burst—so that the slimy yellow oozed over the white—she would cry. And that had happened. The same feeling was upon her now. Gingerly she laid the magazine back on the table and closed her eyes.

The music in the studio seemed to be urging violently and clumsily for something that was not to be had. After a moment her thoughts drew back from Heime and the concerto and the picture—and hovered around the lesson once more. She slid over on the sofa until she could see plainly into the studio—the two of them playing, peering at the notations on the piano, lustfully drawing out all that was there.

She could not forget the memory of Mister Bilderbach's face as he had stared at her a moment ago. Her hands, still twitching unconsciously to the motions of the fugue, closed over her bony knees. Tired, she was. And with a circling, sinking away feeling like the one that often came to her just before she dropped off to sleep on the nights when she had over-practiced. Like those weary half-dreams that buzzed and carried her out into their own whirling space.

A *Wunderkind*—a *Wunderkind*—a *Wunderkind*. The syllables would come out rolling in the deep German way, roar against her ears and then fall to a murmur. Along with the faces circling, swelling out in distortion, diminishing to pale blobs—Mister Bilderbach, Mrs. Bilderbach, Heime, Mister Lafkowitz. Around and around in a circle revolving to the guttural *Wunderkind*. Mister Bilderbach looming large in the middle of the circle, his face urging—with the others around him.

Phrases of music seesawing crazily. Notes she had been practicing falling over each other like a handful of marbles dropped downstairs. Bach, Debussy, Prokofieff, Brahms—timed grotesquely to the far off throb of her tired body and the buzzing circle.

Sometimes—when she had not worked more than three hours or had stayed out from high school—the dreams were not so confused. The music soared clearly in her mind and quick, precise little memories would come back—clear as the sissy "Age of Innocence" picture Heime had given her after their joint concert was over.

A *Wunderkind*—a *Wunderkind*. That was what Mister Bilderbach had called her when, at twelve, she first came to him. Older pupils had repeated the word.

Not that he had ever said the word to her. "Bienchen—" (She had a plain American name but he never used it except when her mistakes were enormous.) "Bienchen," he would say, "I know it must be terrible. Carrying around all the time a head that thick. Poor Bienchen—"

Mister Bilderbach's father had been a Dutch violinist. His mother was from Prague. He had been born in this country and had spent his youth in Germany. So many times she wished she had not been born and brought up in just Cincinnati. How do you say *cheese* in German? Mister Bilderbach, what is Dutch for *I don't understand you?*

The first day she came to the studio. After she played the whole Second Hungarian Rhapsody from memory. The room graying with the twilight. His face as he leaned over the piano.

"Now we begin all over," he said that first day. "It—playing music—is more than cleverness. If a twelve-year-old girl's fingers cover so many keys to a second—that means nothing."

He tapped his broad chest and his forehead with his stubby hand. "Here and here. You are old enough to understand that." He lighted a cigarette and gently blew the first exhalation above her head. "And work—work—work. We will start now with these Bach Inventions and these little Schumann pieces." His hands moved again—this time to jerk the cord of the lamp behind her and point to the music. "I will show you how I wish this practiced. Listen carefully now."

She had been at the piano for almost three hours and was very tired. His deep voice sounded as though it had been straying inside her for a long time. She wanted to reach out and touch his muscle-flexed finger that pointed out the phrases, wanted to feel the gleaming gold band ring and the strong hairy back of his hand.

She had lessons Tuesday after school and on Saturday afternoons. Often she stayed, when the Saturday lesson was finished, for dinner, and then spent the night and took the streetcar home the next morning. Mrs. Bilderbach liked her in her calm, almost dumb way. She was much different from her husband. She was quiet and fat and slow. When she wasn't in the kitchen, cooking the rich dishes that both of them loved, she seemed to spend all her time in their bed upstairs, reading magazines or just looking with a half-smile at nothing. When they had married in Germany she had been a *lieder* singer. She didn't sing any more (she said it was her throat). When he would call her in from the kitchen to listen to a pupil she would always smile and say that it was *gut*, very *gut*.

When Frances was thirteen it came to her one day that the Bilderbachs had no children. It seemed strange. Once she had been back in the kitchen with Mrs. Bilderbach when he had come striding in from the studio, tense with anger at some pupil who had annoyed him. His wife stood stirring the thick soup until his hand groped out and rested on her shoulder. Then she turned—stood placid—while he folded his arms about her and buried his sharp face in the white, nerveless flesh of her neck. They stood that way without moving. And then his face jerked back suddenly, the anger diminished to a quiet inexpressiveness, and he had returned to the studio.

After she had started with Mister Bilderbach and didn't have time to see anything of the people at high school, Heime had been the only friend of her own age. He was Mister Lafkowitz's pupil and would come with him to Mister Bilderbach's on evenings when she would be there. They would listen to their teachers' playing. And often they themselves went over chamber music together—Mozart sonatas or Bloch.

A *Wunderkind*—a *Wunderkind*.

Heime was a *Wunderkind*. He and she, then.

Heime had been playing the violin since he was four. He didn't have to go to school; Mister Lafkowitz's brother, who was crippled, used to teach him geometry and European history and French verbs in the afternoon. When he was thirteen he had as fine a technique as any violinist in Cincinnati—everyone said so. But playing the violin must be easier than the piano. She knew it must be.

Heime always seemed to smell of corduroy pants and the food he had eaten and rosin. Half the time, too, his hands were dirty around the knuckles and the cuffs of his shirts peeped out dingily from the sleeves of his sweater. She always watched his hands when he played—thin only at the joints with the hard little blobs of flesh bulging over the short-cut nails and the babyish-looking crease that showed so plainly in his bowing wrist.

In the dreams, as when she was awake, she could remember the concert only in a blur. She had not known it was unsuccessful for her until months after. True, the papers had praised Heime more than her. But he was much shorter than she. When they stood together on the stage he came only to her shoulders. And that made a difference with people, she knew. Also, there was the matter of the sonata they played together. The Bloch.

"No, no—I don't think that would be appropriate," Mister Bilderbach had said when the Bloch was suggested to end the programme. "Now that John Powell thing—the Sonate Virginianesque."

She hadn't understood then; she wanted it to be the Bloch as much as Mister Lafkowitz and Heime.

Mister Bilderbach had given in. Later, after the reviews had said she lacked the temperament for that type of music, after they called her playing thin and lacking in feeling, she felt cheated.

"That oie oie stuff," said Mister Bilderbach, crackling the newspapers at her. "Not for you, Bienchen. Leave all that to the Heimes and vitses and skys."

A *Wunderkind.* No matter what the papers said, that was what he had called her.

Why was it Heime had done so much better at the concert than she? At school sometimes, when she was supposed to be watching someone do a geometry problem on the blackboard, the question would twist knife-like inside her. She would worry about it in bed, and even sometimes when she was supposed to be concentrating at the piano. It wasn't just the Bloch and her not being Jewish—not entirely. It wasn't that Heime didn't have to go to school and had begun his training so early, either. It was—?

Once she thought she knew.

"Play the Fantasia and Fugue," Mister Bilderbach had demanded one evening a year ago—after he and Mister Lafkowitz had finished reading some music together.

The Bach, as she played, seemed to her well done. From the tail of her eye she could see the calm, pleased expression on Mister Bilderbach's face, see his hands rise climactically from the chair arms and then sink down loose and satisfied when the high points of the phrases had been passed successfully. She stood up from the piano when it was over, swallowing to loosen the bands that the music seemed to have drawn around her throat and chest. But—

"Frances—" Mister Lafkowitz had said then, suddenly, looking at her with his thin mouth curved and his eyes almost covered by their delicate lids. "Do you know how many children Bach had?"

She turned to him, puzzled. "A good many. Twenty some odd."

"Well then—" The corners of his smile etched themselves gently in his pale face. "He could not have been so cold—then."

Mister Bilderbach was not pleased; his guttural effulgence of German words had *Kind* in it somewhere. Mister Lafkowitz raised his eyebrows. She had caught the point easily enough, but she felt no deception in keeping her face blank and immature because that was the way Mister Bilderbach wanted her to look.

Yet such things had nothing to do with it. Nothing very much, at least, for she would grow older. Mister Bilderbach understood that, and even Mister Lafkowitz had not meant just what he said.

In the dreams Mister Bilderbach's face loomed out and contracted in the center of the whirling circle. The lip surging softly, the veins in his temples insisting.

But sometimes, before she slept, there were such clear memories; as when she pulled a hole in the heel of her stocking down, so that her shoe would hide it. "Bienchen, Bienchen!" And bringing Mrs. Bilderbach's work basket in and showing her how it should be darned and not gathered together in a lumpy heap.

And the time she graduated from Junior High.

"What you wear?" asked Mrs. Bilderbach the Sunday morning at breakfast when she told them about how they had practiced to march into the auditorium.

"An evening dress my cousin had last year."

"Ah—Bienchen!" he said, circling his warm coffee cup with his heavy hands, looking up at her with wrinkles around his laughing eyes. "I bet I know what Bienchen wants—"

He insisted. He would not believe her when she explained that she honestly didn't care at all.

"Like this, Anna," he said, pushing his napkin across the table and mincing to the other side of the room, swishing his hips, rolling up his eyes behind his horn-rimmed glasses.

The next Sunday afternoon, after her lessons, he took her to the department stores downtown. His thick fingers smoothed over the filmy nets and crackling taffetas that the saleswomen unwound from their bolts. He held colors to her face, cocking his head to one side, and selected pink. Shoes, he remembered too. He liked best some white kid pumps. They seemed a little like old ladies' shoes to her and the Red Cross label in the instep had a charity look. But it really didn't matter at all. When Mrs. Bilderbach began to cut out the dress and fit it to her with pins, he interrupted his lessons to stand by and suggest ruffles around the hips and neck and a fancy rosette on the shoulder.

The music was coming along nicely thcn. Dresses and commencement and such made no difference.

Nothing mattered much except playing the music as it must be played, bringing out the thing that must be in her, practicing, practicing, playing so that Mister Bilderbach's face lost some of its urging look. Putting the thing into her music that Myra Hess had, and Yehudi Menuhin—even Heime!

What had begun to happen to her four months ago? The notes began springing out with a glib, dead intonation. Adolescence, she thought. Some kids played with promise—and worked and worked until, like her, the least little thing would start them crying, and worn out with trying to get the thing across—the longing thing they felt—something queer began to happen—But not she! She was like Heime. She had to be. She—

Once it was there for sure. And you didn't lose things like that. A *Wunderkind.* . . . A *Wunderkind.* . . . Of her he said it, rolling the words in the sure, deep German way. And in the dreams even deeper, more certain than ever. With his face looming out at her, and the longing phrases of music mixed in with the zooming, circling round, round, round—A *Wunderkind.* A *Wunderkind.* . . .

This afternoon Mister Bilderbach did not show Mister Lafkowitz to the front door, as he usually did. He stayed at the piano, softly pressing a solitary note. Listening, Frances watched the violinist wind his scarf about his pale throat.

"A good picture of Heime," she said, picking up her music. "I got a letter from him a couple of months ago—telling about hearing Schnabel and Huberman and about Carnegie Hall and things to eat at the Russian Tea Room."

To put off going into the studio a moment longer she waited until Mister Lafkowitz was ready to leave and then stood behind him as he opened the door. The frosty cold outside cut into the room. It was growing late and the air was seeped with the pale yellow of winter twilight. When the door swung to on its hinges, the house seemed darker and more silent than ever before she had known it to be.

As she went into the studio Mister Bilderbach got up from the piano and silently watched her settle herself at the keyboard.

"Well, Bienchen," he said, "this afternoon we are going to begin all over. Start from scratch. Forget the last few months."

He looked as though he were trying to act a part in a movie. His solid body swayed from toe to heel, he rubbed his hands together, and even smiled in a satisfied, movie way. Then suddenly he thrust this manner brusquely aside. He heavy shoulders slouched and he began to run through the stack of music she had brought in. "The Bach—no, not yet," he murmured. "The Beethoven? Yes. The Variation Sonata. Opus 26."

The keys of the piano hemmed her in—stiff and white and dead-seeming.

"Wait a minute," he said. He stood in the curve of the piano, elbows propped, and looked at her. "Today I expect something from you. Now this sonata—it's the first Beethoven sonata you ever worked on. Every note is under control—technically—you have nothing to cope with but the music. Only music now. That's all you think about."

He rustled through the pages of her volume until he found the place. Then he pulled his teaching chair halfway across the room, turned it around and seated himself, straddling the back with his legs.

For some reason, she knew, this position of his usually had a good effect on her performance. But today she felt that she would notice him from the corner of her eye and be disturbed. His back was stiffly tilted, his legs looked tense. The heavy volume before him seemed to balance dangerously on the chair back. "Now we begin," he said with a peremptory dart of his eyes in her direction.

Her hands rounded over the keys and then sank down. The first notes were too loud, the other phrases followed dryly.

Arrestingly his hand rose up from the score. "Wait! Think a minute what you're playing. How is this beginning marked?"

"An—andante."

"All right. Don't drag it into an *adagio* then. And play deeply into the keys. Don't snatch it off shallowly that way. A graceful, deep-toned *andante*—"

She tried again. Her hands seemed separate from the music that was in her.

"Listen," he interrupted. "Which of these variations dominates the whole?"

"The dirge," she answered.

"Then prepare for that. This is an *andante*—but it's not salon stuff as you just played it. Start out softly, *piano*, and make it swell out just before the arpeggio. Make it warm and dramatic.

And down here—where it's marked *dolce* make the counter melody sing out. You know all that. We've gone over all that side of it before. Now play it. Feel it as Beethoven wrote it down. Feel that tragedy and restraint."

She could not stop looking at his hands. They seemed to rest tentatively on the music, ready to fly up as a stop signal as soon as she would begin, the gleaming flash of his ring calling her to halt. "Mister Bilderbach—maybe if I—if you let me play on through the first variation without stopping I could do better."

"I won't interrupt," he said.

Her pale face leaned over too close to the keys. She played through the first part, and, obeying a nod from him, began the second. There were no flaws that jarred on her, but the phrases shaped from her fingers before she had put into them the meaning that she felt.

When she had finished he looked up from the music and began to speak with dull bluntness: "I hardly heard those harmonic fillings in the right hand. And incidentally, this part was supposed to take on intensity, develop the foreshadowings that were supposed to be inherent in the first part. Go on with the next one, though."

She wanted to start it with subdued viciousness and progress to a feeling of deep, swollen sorrow. Her mind told her that. But her hands seemed to gum in the keys like limp macaroni and she could not imagine the music as it should be.

When the last note had stopped vibrating, he closed the book and deliberately got up from the chair. He was moving his lower jaw from side to side—and between his open lips she could glimpse the pink healthy lane to his throat and his strong, smoke-yellowed teeth. He laid the Beethoven gingerly on top of the rest of her music and propped his elbows on the smooth, black piano top once more. "No," he said simply, looking at her.

Her mouth began to quiver. "I can't help it. I—"

Suddenly he strained his lips into a smile. "Listen, Bienchen," he began in a new, forced voice. "You still play the Harmonious Blacksmith, don't you? I told you not to drop it from your repertoire."

"Yes," she said. "I practice it now and then."

His voice was the one he used for children. "It was among the first things we worked on together—remember. So strongly you used to play it—like a real blacksmith's daughter. You see, Bienchen, I know you so well—as if you were my own girl. I know what you have—I've heard you play so many things beautifully. You used to—"

He stopped in confusion and inhaled from his pulpy stub of cigarette. The smoke drowsed out from his pink lips and clung in a gray mist around the lank hair and childish forehead.

"Make it happy and simple," he said, switching on the lamp behind her and stepping back from the piano.

For a moment he stood just inside the bright circle the light made. Then impulsively he squatted down to the floor. "Vigorous," he said.

She could not stop looking at him, sitting on one heel with the other foot resting squarely before him for balance, the muscles of his strong thighs straining under the cloth of his trousers, his back straight, his elbows staunchly propped on his knees. "Simply now," he repeated with a gesture of his fleshy hands. "Think of the blacksmith—working out in the sunshine all day. Working easily and undisturbed."

She could not look down at the piano. The light brightened the hairs on the backs of his outspread hands, made the lenses of his glasses glitter.

"All of it," he urged. "Now!"

She felt that the marrows of her bones were hollow and there was no blood left in her. Her heart that had been springing against her chest all afternoon felt suddenly dead. She saw it gray and limp and shriveled at the edges like an oyster.

His face seemed to throb out in space before her, come closer with the lurching motion in the veins of his temples. In retreat, she looked down at the piano. Her lips shook like jelly and a surge of noiseless tears made the white keys blur in a watery line. "I can't," she whispered. "I don't know why, but I just can't—can't any more."

His tense body slackened and, holding his hand to his side, he pulled himself up. She clutched her music and hurried past him.

Her coat. The mittens and galoshes. The schoolbooks and the satchel he had given her on her birthday. All from the silent room that was hers. Quickly—before she would have to speak.

As she passed through the vestibule she could not help but see his hands—held out from his body that leaned against the studio door, relaxed and purposeless. The door shut to firmly. Dragging her books and satchel she stumbled down the stone steps, turned in the wrong direction, and hurried down the street that had become confused with noise and bicycles and the games of other children.

from

River of Earth

James Still

THE mines on Little Carr closed in March. Winter had been mild, the snows scant and frost-thin upon the ground. Robins stayed the season through, and sapsuckers came early to drill the black birch beside our house. Though Father had worked in the mines, we did not live in the camps. He owned the scrap of land our house stood upon, a garden patch, and the black birch that was the only tree on all the barren slope above Blackjack. There were three of us children running barefoot over the puncheon floors, and since the year's beginning Mother carried a fourth balanced on one hip as she worked over the rusty stove in the shedroom. There were eight in the family to cook for. Two of Father's cousins, Harl and Tibb Logan, came with the closing of the mines and did not go away.

"It's all we can do to keep bread in the children's mouths," Mother told Father. "Even if they are your blood kin, we can't feed them much longer." Mother knew the strings of shucky beans dried in the fall would not last until a new garden could be raised. A half-dozen soup bones and some meat rinds were left in the smokehouse; skippers had got into a pork shoulder during the unnaturally warm December, and it had to be thrown away. Mother ate just enough for the baby, picking at her food and chewing it in little bites. Father ate sparingly, cleaning his plate of every crumb. His face was almost thin as Mother's. Harl and Tibb fed well, and grumblingly, upon beans and corn pone. They kicked each other under the table, carrying on a secret joke from day to day, and grimacing at us as they ate. We were pained, and felt foolish because we could not join in their laughter. "You'll have to ask them to go," Mother told Father. "These lazy louts are taking food out of the baby's mouth. What we have won't last forever." Father did not speak for a long time; then he said simply: "I can't turn my kin out." He would say no more. Mother began to feed us between meals, putting less on the table. They would chuckle without saying anything. Sometimes one of them would make a clucking noise in his throat, but none of us laughed, not even Euly. We would look at Father, his chin drooped over his shirt collar, his eyes lowered. And Fletch's face would be as grave as Father's. Only the baby's face would become bird-eyed and bright.

When Uncle Samp, Father's great-uncle, came for a couple of days and stayed on after the week-end was over, Mother spoke sternly to Father. Father became angry and stamped his foot on the floor. "As long as we've got a crust, it'll never be said I turned my folks from my door," he said. We children were frightened. We had never seen Father storm like this, or heard him raise his voice at Mother. Father was so angry he took his rifle-gun and went off into the woods for the day, bringing in four squirrels for supper. He had barked them, firing at the tree trunk beside the animals' heads, and bringing them down without a wound.

Uncle Samp was a large man. His skin was soft and white, with small pink veins webbing his cheeks and nose. There were no powder burns on his face and hands, and no coal dust ground into the heavy wrinkles of his neck. He had a thin gray mustache, over a hand-span in length, wrapped like a loose cord around his ears. He vowed it had not been trimmed in thirty years. It put a spell on us all, Father's cousins included. We looked at the mustache and felt an itching uneasiness. That night at the table Harl and Tibb ate squirrels' breasts and laughed, winking at each other as they brushed up brown gravy on pieces of corn pone. Uncle Samp told us what this good eating put him in mind of, and he bellowed, his laughter coming deep out of him. The rio lamp trembled on the table. We laughed, watching his face redden with every gust, watching the mustache hang miraculously over his ears. Suddenly my brother Fletch began to cry over his plate. His shins had been kicked under the table. Mother's face paled, her eyes becoming hard and dark. She gave the baby to Father and took Fletch into another room. We ate quietly during the rest of the meal, Father looking sternly down the table.

After supper Mother and Father took a lamp and went out to the smokehouse. We followed, finding them bent over the meat box. Father dug into the salt with a plow blade, Mother holding the light above him. He uncovered three curled rinds of pork. We stayed in the smokehouse a long time, feeling contented and together. The room was large, and we jumped around like savages and swung head-down from the rafters.

Father crawled around on his hands and knees with the baby on his back. Mother sat on a sack of black walnuts and watched us. "Hit's the first time we've been alone in two months," she said. "If we lived in here, there wouldn't be room for anybody else. And it would be healthier than that leaky shack we stay in." Father kept crawling with the baby, kicking up his feet like a spoiled nag. Fletch hurt his leg again. He gritted his teeth and showed us the purple spot where he had been kicked. Father rubbed the bruise and made it feel better. "Their hearts are black as Satan," Mother said. "I'd rather live in this smokehouse than stay down there with them. A big house draws kinfolks like a horse draws nitflies."

It was late when we went to the house. The sky was overcast and starless. During the night, rain came suddenly, draining through the rotten shingles. Father got up in the dark and pushed the beds about. He bumped against a footboard and wakened me. I heard Uncle Samp snoring in the next room; and low and indistinct through the sound of water on the roof came the quiver of laughter. Harl and Tibb were awake in the next room. They were mightily tickled about something. They laughed in long, choking spasms. The sound came to me as though afar off, and I reckon they had their heads under the covers so as not to waken Uncle Samp. I listened and wondered how it was possible to laugh with all the dark and rain.

Morning was bright and rain-fresh. The sharp sunlight fell slantwise upon the worn limestone earth of the hills, and our house squatted weathered and dark on the bald slope. Yellow-bellied sapsuckers drilled their oblong holes in the black birch by the house, now leafing from tight-curled buds. Fletch and I had climbed into the tree before breakfast, and when Mother called us in we were hungry for our boiled wheat.

We were alone at the table, Harl and Tibb having left at daylight for Blackjack. They had left without their breakfast, and this haste seemed strange to Mother. "This is the first meal they've missed," she said.

Uncle Samp slept on in the next room, his head buried under a quilt to keep the light out of his face. Mother fed the baby at her breast, standing by Father at the table. We ate our wheat without sugar, and when we had finished, Mother said to Father: "We have enough bran for three more pans of bread. If the children eat it by themselves, it might last a week. It won't last us all more than three meals. Your kin will have to go today."

Father put his spoon down with a clatter. "My folks eat when we eat," he said, "and as long as we eat." The corners of his mouth were drawn tight into his face. His eyes burned, but there was no anger in them. "I'll get some meal at the store," he said.

Mother leaned against the wall, clutching the baby. Her voice was like ice. "They won't let you have it on credit. You've tried before. We've got to live small. We've got to start over again, hand to mouth, the way we began." She laid her hand upon the air, marking the words with nervous fingers. "We've got to tie ourselves up in such a knot nobody else can get in." Father got his hat and stalked to the door. "We've got to do hit today," she called. But Father was gone, out of the house and over the hill toward Blackjack.

Mother put the baby in the empty wood box while she washed dishes. Euly helped her, clearing the table and setting out a bowl of boiled wheat for Uncle Samp. I went outside with Fletch, and we were driving the sapsuckers from the birch when Uncle Samp shouted in the house. His voice crashed through the wall, pouring between the seamy timbers in raw blasts of anger. Fletch was up in the tree, near the tiptop, so I ran ahead of him into the shedroom. Mother stood in the middle of the floor listening. Baby Green jumped up and down in the wood box. Euly ran behind the stove.

I ran into the room where Uncle Samp was and saw him stride from the looking glass to the bed. His mouth was slack. A low growl flowed out of him. He stopped when he saw me, drawing himself up in his wrath. Then I saw his face, and I was frightened. I was suddenly paralyzed with fear. His face was fiery, the red web of veins straining in this flesh, and his mustache, which had been cut off within an inch of his lips, sticking out like to small gray horns. He rushed upon me, caught me up in his arms, and flung me against the wall. I fell upon the floor, breathless, not uttering a sound. Mother was beside me in a moment, her hands weak and palsied as she lifted me.

I was only frightened, and not hurt. Mother cried a little, making a dry sniffling sound through her nose; then she got up and walked outside and around the house. Uncle Samp was not in sight. She came back and gave Fletch the key to the smokehouse. "We're going to move up there," she said. "Go unlock the door." I helped Euly carry the baby out in the wood box. We set him on the shady side of the woodpile. We began to move the furniture, putting the smaller things in the smokehouse, but leaving the chairs, beds, and tables on the ground halfway between. The stove was heaviest of all, and still hot. The rusty legs broke off on one side, and the other two bent under it. We managed to slide it into the yard. Mother carried the clock and the rio lamp to the smokehouse.The clock rattled with four pennies Fletch kept inside it.

After everything had been taken out we waited in the backyard while Mother went around the house again, looking off the hill. Uncle Samp was nowhere in sight, and neither Harl nor Tibb could be seen. Then she went inside alone. She stayed a long time. We could hear her moving across the floor. When she came out and closed the door there was a haze of smoke behind her, blue and smelling of burnt wood.

In a moment we saw the flames through the back window. The rooms were lighted up, and fire ran up the walls, eating into the old timbers. It climbed to the ceiling, burst through the roof, and ate the rotten shingles like leaves. Fletch and I watched the sapsuckers fly in noisy haste from the black birch, and he began to cry hoarsely as the young leaves wilted and hung limp from scorched twigs. The birch trunk steamed in the heat.

When the flames were highest, leaping through the charred rafters, a gun fired repeatedly in the valley. Someone there had noticed the smoke and was arousing the folk along Little Carr Creek. When they arrived, the walls had fallen in, and Mother stood among the scattered furnishings, her face calm and triumphant.

A Visit of Charity

Eudora Welty

IT was mid-morning—a very cold, bright day. Holding a potted plant before her, a girl of fourteen jumped off the bus in front of the Old Ladies' Home, on the outskirts of town. She wore a red coat, and her straight yellow hair was hanging down loose from the pointed white cap all the little girls were wearing that year. She stopped for a moment beside one of the prickly dark shrubs with which the city had beautified the Home, and then proceeded slowly toward the building, which was of whitewashed brick and reflected the winter sunlight like a block of ice. As she walked vaguely up the steps she shifted the small pot from hand to hand; then she had to set it down and remove her mittens before she could open the heavy door.

"I'm a Campfire Girl. . . . I have to pay a visit to some old lady," she told the nurse at the desk. This was a woman in a white uniform who looked as if she were cold; she had close-cut hair which stood up on the very top of her head exactly like a sea wave. Marian, the little girl, did not tell her that this visit would give her a minimum of only three points in her score.

"Acquainted with any of our residents?" asked the nurse. She lifted one eyebrow and spoke like a man.

"With any old ladies? No—but—that is, any of them will do," Marian stammered. With her free hand she pushed her hair behind her ears, as she did when it was time to study Science.

The nurse shrugged and rose. "You have a nice *multiflora cineraria* there," she remarked as she walked ahead down the hall of closed doors to pick out an old lady.

There was loose, bulging linoleum on the floor. Marian felt as if she were walking on the waves, but the nurse paid no attention to it. There was a smell in the hall like the interior of a clock. Everything was silent until, behind one of the doors, an old lady of some kind cleared her throat like a sheep bleating. This decided the nurse. Stopping in her tracks, she first extended her arm, bent her elbow, and leaned forward from the hips—all to examine the watch strapped to her wrist; then she gave a loud double-rap on the door.

"There are two in each room," the nurse remarked over her shoulder.

"Two what?" asked Marian without thinking. The sound like a sheep's bleating almost made her turn around and run back.

One old woman was pulling the door open in short, gradual jerks, and when she saw the nurse a strange smile forced her old face dangerously awry. Marian, suddenly propelled by the strong, impatient arm of the nurse, saw next the side-face of another old woman, even older, who was lying flat in bed with a cap on and a counterpane drawn up to her chin.

"Visitor," said the nurse, and after one more shove she was off up the hall.

Marian stood tongue-tied; both hands held the potted plant. The old woman, still with that terrible, square smile (which was a smile of welcome) stamped on her bony face, was waiting. . . . Perhaps she said something. The old woman in bed said nothing at all, and she did not look around.

Suddenly Marian saw a hand, quick as a bird claw, reach up in the air and pluck the white cap off her head. At the same time, another claw to match drew her all the way into the room, and the next moment the door closed behind her.

"My, my, my," said the old lady at her side.

Marian stood enclosed by a bed, a washstand and a chair; the tiny room had altogether too much furniture. Everything smelled wet—even the bare floor. She held on to the back of the chair, which was wicker and felt soft and damp. Her heart beat more and more slowly, her hands got colder and colder, and she could not hear whether the old women were saying anything or not. She could not see them very clearly. How dark it was! The window shade was down, and the only door was shut. Marian looked at the ceiling. . . . It was like being caught in a robbers' cave, just before one was murdered.

"Did you come to be our little girl for a while?" the first robber asked.

Then something was snatched from Marian's hand—the little potted plant.

"Flowers!" screamed the old woman. She stood holding the pot in an undecided way. "Pretty flowers," she added.

Then the old woman in bed cleared her throat and spoke. "They are not pretty," she said, still without looking around, but very distinctly.

Marian suddenly pitched against the chair and sat down in it.

"Pretty flowers," the first old woman insisted. "Pretty— pretty . . ."

Marian wished she had the little pot back for just a moment—she had forgotten to look at the plant herself before giving it away. What did it look like?

"Stinkweeds," said the other old woman sharply. She had a bunchy white forehead and red eyes like a sheep. Now she turned them toward Marian. The fogginess seemed to rise in her throat again, and she bleated, "Who—are—you?"

To her surprise, Marian could not remember her name. "I'm a Campfire Girl," she said finally.

"Watch out for the germs," said the old woman like a sheep, not addressing anyone.

"One came out last month to see us," said the first old woman.

A sheep or a germ? wondered Marian dreamily, holding on to the chair.

"Did not!" cried the other old woman.

"Did so! Read to us out of the Bible, and we enjoyed it!" screamed the first.

"Who enjoyed it!" said the woman in bed. Her mouth was unexpectedly small and sorrowful, like a pet's.

"We enjoyed it," insisted the other. "You enjoyed it—I enjoyed it."

"We all enjoyed it," said Marian, without realizing that she had said a word.

The first old woman had just finished putting the potted plant high, high on the top of the wardrobe, where it could hardly be seen from below. Marian wondered how she had ever succeeded in placing it there, how she could ever have reached so high.

"You mustn't pay any attention to old Addie," she now said to the little girl. "She's ailing today."

"Will you shut your mouth?" said the woman in bed. "I am not."

"You're a story."

"I can't stay but a minute—really, I can't," said Marian suddenly. She looked down at the wet floor and thought that if she were sick in here they would have to let her go.

With much to-do the first old woman sat down in a rocking chair—still another piece of furniture!—and began to rock. With the fingers of one hand she touched a very dirty cameo pin on her chest. "What do you do at school?" she asked.

"I don't know . . ." said Marian. She tried to think but she could not.

"Oh, but the flowers are beautiful," the old woman whispered. She seemed to rock faster and faster; Marian did not see how anyone could rock so fast.

"Ugly," said the woman in bed.

"If we bring flowers—" Marian began, and then fell silent. She had almost said that if Campfire Girls brought flowers to the Old Ladies' Home, the visit would count one extra point, and if they took a Bible with them on the bus and read it to the old ladies, it counted double. But the old woman had not listened, anyway; she was rocking and watching the other one, who watched back from the bed.

"Poor Addie is ailing. She has to take medicine—see?" she said, pointing a horny finger at a row of bottles on the table, and rocking so high that her black comfort shoes lifted off the floor like a little child's.

"I am no more sick than you are," said the woman in bed.

"Oh, yes you are!"

"I just got more sense than you have, that's all," said the other old woman, nodding her head.

"That's only the contrary way she talks when *you all* come," said the first old lady with sudden intimacy. She stopped the rocker with a neat pat of her feet and leaned toward Marian. Her hand reached over—it felt like a petunia leaf, clinging and just a little sticky.

"Will you hush! Will you hush!" cried the other one.

Marian leaned back rigidly in her chair.

"When I was a little girl like you, I went to school and all," said the old woman in the same intimate, menacing voice. "Not here—another town . . ."

"Hush!" said the sick woman. "You never went to school. You never came and you never went. You never were anything—only here. You never were born! You don't know anything. Your head is empty, your heart and hands and your old black purse are all empty, even that little old box that you brought with you you brought empty—you showed it to me. And yet you talk, talk, talk, talk, talk all the time until I think I'm losing my mind! Who are you? You're a stranger—a perfect stranger! Don't you know you're a stranger? Is it possible that they have actually done a thing like this to anyone—sent them in a stranger to talk, and rock, and tell away her whole long rigmarole? Do they seriously suppose that I'll be able to keep it up, day in, day out, night in, night out, living in the same room with a terrible old woman—forever?"

Marian saw the old woman's eyes grow bright and turn toward her. This old woman was looking at her with despair and calculation in her face. Her small lips suddenly dropped apart, and exposed a half circle of false teeth with tan gums.

"Come here, I want to tell you something," she whispered. "Come here!"

Marian was trembling, and her heart nearly stopped beating altogether for a moment.

"Now, now, Addie," said the first old woman. "That's not polite. Do you know what's really the matter with old Addie today?" She, too, looked at Marian; one of her eyelids dropped low.

"The matter?" the child repeated stupidly. "What's the matter with her?"

"Why, she's mad because it's her birthday!" said the first old woman, beginning to rock again and giving a little crow as though she had answered her own riddle.

"It is not, it is not!" screamed the old woman in bed. "It is not my birthday, no one knows when that is but myself, and will you please be quiet and say nothing more, or I'll go straight out of my mind!" She turned her eyes toward Marian again, and presently she said in the soft, foggy voice, "When the worst comes to the worst, I ring this bell, and the nurse comes." One of her hands was drawn out from under the patched counterpane—a thin little hand with enormous black freckles. With a finger which would not hold still she pointed to a little bell on the table among the bottles.

"How old are you?" Marian breathed. Now she could see the old woman in bed very closely and plainly, and very abruptly, from all sides, as in dreams. She wondered about her—she wondered for a moment as though there was nothing else in the world to wonder about. It was the first time such a thing had happened to Marian.

"I won't tell!"

The old face on the pillow, where Marian was bending over it, slowly gathered and collapsed. Soft whimpers came out of the small open mouth. It was a sheep that she sounded like—a little lamb. Marian's face drew very close, the yellow hair hung forward.

"She's crying!" She turned a bright, burning face up to the first old woman.

"That's Addie for you," the old woman said spitefully.

Marian jumped up and moved toward the door. For the second time, the claw almost touched her hair, but it was not quick enough. The little girl put her cap on.

"Well, it was a real visit," said the old woman, following Marian through the doorway and all the way out into the hall. Then from behind she suddenly clutched the child with her sharp little fingers. In an affected, high-pitched whine she cried, "Oh, little girl, have you a penny to spare for a poor old woman that's not got anything of her own? We don't have a thing in the world—not a penny for candy—not a thing! Little girl, just a nickel—a penny—"

Marian pulled violently against the old hands for a moment before she was free. Then she ran down the hall, without looking behind her and without looking at the nurse, who was reading *Field & Stream* at her desk. The nurse, after another triple motion to consult her wrist watch, asked automatically the question put to visitors in all institutions: "Won't you stay and have dinner with *us*?"

Marian never replied. She pushed the heavy door open into the cold air and ran down the steps.

Under the prickly shrub she stopped and quickly, without being seen, retrieved a red apple she had hidden there.

Her yellow hair under the white cap, her scarlet coat, her bare knees all flashed in the sunlight as she ran to meet the big bus rocketing through the street.

"Wait for me!" she shouted. As though at an imperial command, the bus ground to a stop.

She jumped on and took a big bite out of the apple.

Childhood

Margaret Walker

When I was a child I knew red miners
dressed raggedly and wearing carbide lamps.
I saw them come down red hills to their camps
dyed with red dust from old Ishkooda mines.
Night after night I met them on the roads,
or on the streets in town I caught their glance;
the swing of dinner buckets in their hands,
and grumbling undermining all their words.

I also lived in low cotton country
where moonlight hovered over ripe haystacks,
or stumps of trees, and croppers' rotting shacks
with famine, terror, flood, and plague near by;
where sentiment and hatred still held sway
and only bitter land was washed away.

Another April

Jesse Stuart

"NOW, Pap, you won't get cold," Mom said as she put a heavy wool cap over his head.

"Huh, what did ye say?" Grandpa asked, holding his big hand cupped over his ear to catch the sound.

"Wait until I get your gloves," Mom said, hollering real loud in Grandpa's ear. Mom had forgotten about his gloves until he raised his big bare hand above his ear to catch the sound of Mom's voice.

"Don't get 'em," Grandpa said, "I won't ketch cold."

Mom didn't pay any attention to what Grandpa said. She went on to get the gloves anyway. Grandpa turned toward me. He saw that I was looking at him.

"Yer Ma's a-puttin' enough clothes on me to kill a man," Grandpa said, then he laughed a coarse laugh like March wind among the pine tops at his own words. I started laughing but not at Grandpa's words. He thought I was laughing at them and we both laughed together. It pleased Grandpa to think that I had laughed with him over something funny that he had said. But I was laughing at the way he was dressed. He looked like a picture of Santa Claus. But Grandpa's cheeks were not cherry-red like Santa Claus' cheeks. They were covered with white thin beard—and above his eyes were long white eyebrows almost as white as percoon petals and very much longer.

Grandpa was wearing a heavy wool suit that hung loosely about his big body but fitted him tightly round the waist where he was as big and as round as a flour barrel. His pant legs were as big 'round his pipestem legs as emptied meal sacks. And his big shoes, with his heavy wool socks dropping down over their tops, looked like sled runners. Grandpa wore a heavy wool shirt and over his wool shirt he wore a heavy wool sweater and then his coat over the top of all this. Over his coat he wore a heavy overcoat and about his neck he wore a wool scarf.

The way Mom had dressed Grandpa you'd think there was a heavy snow on the ground but there wasn't. April was here in-stead and the sun was shining on the green hills where the wild plums and the wild crab apples were in bloom enough to make you think there were big snowdrifts sprinkled over the green hills. When I looked at Grandpa and then looked out at the window at the sunshine and the green grass I laughed more. Grandpa laughed with me.

"I'm a-goin' to see my old friend," Grandpa said just as Mom came down the stairs with his gloves.

"Who is he, Grandpa?" I asked, but Grandpa just looked at my mouth working. He didn't know what I was saying. And he hated to ask me the second time.

Mom put the big wool gloves on Grandpa's hands. He stood there just like I had to do years ago, and let Mom put his gloves on. If Mom didn't get his fingers back in the glove-fingers exactly right Grandpa quarreled at Mom. And when Mom fixed his fingers exactly right in his gloves the way he wanted them Grandpa was pleased.

"I'll be a-goin' to see 'im," Grandpa said to Mom. "I know he'll still be there."

Mom opened our front door for Grandpa and he stepped out slowly, supporting himself with his big cane in one hand. With the other hand he held to the door facing. Mom let him out of the house just like she used to let me out in the spring. And when Grandpa left the house I wanted to go with him, but Mom wouldn't let me go. I wondered if he would get away from the house—get out of Mom's sight—and pull off his shoes and go barefooted and wade the creeks like I used to do when Mom let me out. Since Mom wouldn't let me go with Grandpa, I watched him as he walked slowly down the path in front of our house. Mom stood there watching Grandpa too. I think she was afraid that he would fall. But Mom was fooled; Grandpa toddled along the path better than my baby brother could.

"He used to be a powerful man," Mom said more to herself than she did to me. "He was a timber cutter. No man could cut more timber than my father; no man in the timber woods could sink an ax deeper into a log than my father. And no man could lift the end of a bigger saw log than Pap could."

"Who is Grandpa goin' to see, Mom?" I asked.

"He's not goin' to see anybody," Mom said.

"I heard 'im say that he was goin' to see an old friend," I told her.

"Oh, he was just a-talkin'," Mom said.

I watched Grandpa stop under the pine tree in our front yard. He set his cane against the pine tree trunk, pulled off his gloves and put them in his pocket. Then Grandpa stooped over slowly, as slowly as the wind bends down a sapling, and picked up a pine cone in his big soft fingers. Grandpa stood fondling the pine cone in his hand. Then, one by one, he pulled the little chips from the pine cone—tearing it to pieces like he was hunting for something in it—and after he had torn it to pieces he threw the pine-cone stem on the ground. Then he pulled pine needles from a low-hanging pine bough and he felt of each pine needle between his fingers. He played with them a long time before he started down the path.

"What's Grandpa doin'?" I ask Mom.

But Mom didn't answer me.

"How long has Grandpa been with us?" I asked Mom.

"Before you's born," she said. "Pap has been with us eleven years. He was eighty when he quit cuttin' timber and farmin'; now he's ninety-one."

I had heard her say that when she was a girl he'd walk out on the snow and ice barefooted and carry wood in the house and put it on the fire. He had shoes but he wouldn't bother to put them on. And I heard her say that he would cut timber on the coldest days without socks on his feet but with his feet stuck down in cold brogan shoes and he worked stripped above the waist so his arms would have freedom when he swung his double-bitted ax. I had heard her tell how he'd sweat and how the sweat in his beard would be icicles by the time he got home from work on the cold winter days. Now Mom wouldn't let him get out of the house for she wanted him to live a long time.

As I watched Grandpa go down the path toward the hog pen he stopped to examine every little thing along his path. Once he waved his cane at a butterfly as it zigzagged over his head, its polka-dot wings fanning the blue April air. Grandpa would stand when a puff of wind came along, and hold his face against the wind and let the wind play with his white whiskers. I thought maybe his face was hot under his beard and he was letting the wind cool his face. When he reached the hog pen he called the hogs down to the fence. They came running and grunting to Grandpa just like they were talking to him. I knew that Grandpa couldn't hear them trying to talk to him but he could see their mouths working and he knew they were trying to say something. He leaned his cane against the hog pen, reached over the fence, and patted the hogs' heads. Grandpa didn't miss patting one of our seven hogs.

As he toddled up the little path alongside the hog pen he stopped under a blooming dogwood. He pulled a white blossom from a bough that swayed over the path above his head, and he leaned his big bundled body against the dogwood while he tore each petal from the blossom and examined it carefully. There wasn't anything his dim blue eyes missed. He stopped under a redbud tree before he reached the garden to break a tiny spray of redbud blossoms. He took each blossom from the spray and examined it carefully.

"Gee, it's funny to watch Grandpa," I said to Mom, then I laughed.

"Poor Pap," Mom said, "he's seen a lot of Aprils come and go. He's seen more Aprils than he will ever see again."

I don't think Grandpa missed a thing on the little circle he took before he reached the house. He played with a bumblebee that was bending a windflower blossom that grew near our corn-crib beside a big bluff. But Grandpa didn't try to catch the bumblebee in his big bare hand. I wondered if he would and if the bumblebee would sting him, and if he would holler. Grandpa even pulled a butterfly cocoon from a blackberry briar that grew beside his path. I saw him try to tear it into shreds but he couldn't. There wasn't any butterfly in it, for I'd seen it before. I wondered if the butterfly with the polka-dot wings, that Grandpa waved his cane at when he first left the house, had come from this cocoon. I laughed when Grandpa couldn't tear the cocoon apart.

"I'll bet I can tear that cocoon apart for Grandpa if you'd let me go help him," I said to Mom.

"You leave your Grandpa alone," Mom said. "Let 'im enjoy April."

Then I knew that this was the first time Mom had let Grandpa out of the house all winter. I knew that Grandpa loved the sun-shine and the fresh April air that blew from the redbud and dog-wood blossoms. He loved the bumblebees, the hogs, the pine cones, and pine needles. Grandpa didn't miss a thing along his walk. And every day from now on until just before frost Grandpa would take this little walk. He'd stop along and look at every-thing as he had done summers before. But each year he didn't take as long a walk as he had taken the year before. Now this spring he didn't go down to the lower end of the hog pen as he had done last year. And when I could first remember Grandpa going on his walks he used to go out of sight. He'd go all over the farm. And he'd come to the house and take me on his knee and tell about all what he had seen. Now Grandpa wasn't getting out of sight. I could see him from the window along all of his walk.

Grandpa didn't come back into the house at the front door. He tottled around back of the house toward the smokehouse and I ran through the living room to the dining room so I could look out at the window and watch him.

"Where's Grandpa goin'?" I ask Mom.

"Now never mind," Mom said. "Leave your Grandpa alone. Don't go out there and disturb him."

"I won't bother 'im, Mom," I said. "I just want to watch 'im."

"All right," Mom said.

But Mom wanted to be sure that I didn't bother him so she followed me into the dining room. Maybe she wanted to see what Grandpa was going to do. She stood by the window and we watched Grandpa as he walked down beside our smokehouse where a tall sassafras tree's thin leaves fluttered in the blue April wind. Above the smokehouse and the tall sassafras was a blue April sky—so high you couldn't see the sky-roof. It was just blue space and little white clouds floated upon this blue.

When Grandpa reached the smokehouse he leaned his cane against the sassafras tree. He let himself down slowly to his knees as he looked carefully at the ground. Grandpa was looking at something and I wondered what it was. I just didn't think or I would have known.

"There you are, my good old friend," Grandpa said.

"Who is his friend, Mom?" I asked.

Mom didn't say anything. Then I saw.

"He's playin' with that old terrapin, Mom," I said.

"I know he is," Mom said.

"The terrapin doesn't mind if Grandpa strokes his head with his hand," I said.

"I know it," Mom said.

"But the old terrapin won't let me do it," I said. "Why does he let Grandpa?"

"The terrapin knows your Grandpa."

"He ought to know me," I said, "but when I try to stroke his head with my hand, he closes up in his shell."

Mom didn't say anything. She stood by the window watching Grandpa and listening to Grandpa talk to the terrapin.

"My old friend, how do you like the sunshine?" Grandpa asked the terrapin.

The terrapin turned his fleshless face to one side like a hen does when she looks at you in the sunlight. He was trying to talk to Grandpa; maybe the terrapin could understand what Grandpa was saying.

"Old fellow, it's been a hard winter," Grandpa said. "How have you fared under the smokehouse floor?"

"Does the terrapin know what Grandpa is sayin'?" I asked Mom.

"I don't know," she said.

"I'm awfully glad to see you, old fellow," Grandpa said.

He didn't offer to bite Grandpa's big soft hand as he stroked his head.

"Looks like the terrapin would bite Grandpa," I said.

"That terrapin has spent the winters under that smokehouse for fifteen years," Mom said. "Pap has been acquainted with him for eleven years. He's been talkin' to that terrapin every spring."

"How does Grandpa know the terrapin is old?" I asked Mom.

"It's got 1847 cut on its shell," Mom said. "We know he's ninety-five years old. He's older than that. We don't know how old he was when that date was cut on his back."

"Who cut 1847 on his back, Mom?"

"I don't know, child," she said, "but I'd say whoever cut that date on his back has long been under the ground."

Then I wondered how a terrapin could get that old and what kind of a looking person he was who cut the date on the terrapin's back. I wondered where it happened—if it happened near where our house stood. I wondered who lived here on this land then, what kind of a house they lived in, and if they had a sassafras with tiny thin April leaves on its top growing in their yard, and if the person that cut the date on the terrapin's back was buried at Plum Grove, if he had farmed these hills where we lived today and cut timber like Grandpa had—and if he had seen the Aprils pass like Grandpa had seen them and if he enjoyed them like Grandpa was enjoying this April. I wondered if he had looked at the dogwood blossoms, the redbud blossoms, and talked to this same terrapin.

"Are you well, old fellow?" Grandpa asked the terrapin.

The terrapin just looked at Grandpa.

"I'm well as common for a man of my age," Grandpa said.

"Did the terrapin ask Grandpa if he was well?" I asked Mom.

"I don't know," Mom said. "I can't talk to a terrapin."

"But Grandpa can."

"Yes."

"Wait until tomatoes get ripe and we'll go to the garden together," Grandpa said.

"Does a terrapin eat tomatoes?" I asked Mom.

"Yes, that terrapin has been eatin' tomatoes from our garden for fifteen years," Mom said. "When Mick was tossin' the terrapins out of the tomato patch, he picked up this one and found the date cut on his back. He put him back in the patch and told him to help himself. He lives from our garden every year. We don't bother him and don't allow anybody else to bother him. He spends his winters under our smokehouse floor buried in the dry ground."

"Gee, Grandpa looks like the terrapin," I said.

Mom didn't say anything; tears came to her eyes. She wiped them from her eyes with the corner of her apron.

"I'll be back to see you," Grandpa said. "I'm a-gettin' a little chilly; I'll be gettin' back to the house."

The terrapin twisted his wrinkled neck without moving his big body, poking his head deeper into the April wind as Grandpa pulled his bundled body up by holding to the sassafras tree trunk.

"Good-bye, old friend!"

The terrapin poked his head deeper into the wind, holding one eye on Grandpa, for I could see his eye shining in the sinking sunlight.

Grandpa got his cane that was leaned against the sassafras tree trunk and hobbled slowly toward the house. The terrapin looked at him with first one eye then the other.

The Crop

Flannery O'Connor

MISS Willerton always crumbed the table. It was her particular household accomplishment and she did it with great thoroughness. Lucia and Bertha did the dishes and Garner went into the parlor and did the *Morning Press* crossword puzzle. That left Miss Willerton in the dining room by herself and that was all right with Miss Willerton. Whew! Breakfast in that house was always an ordeal. Lucia insisted that they have a regular hour for breakfast just like they did for other meals. Lucia said a regular breakfast made for other regular habits, and with Garner's tendency to upsets, it was imperative that they establish some system in their eating. This way she could also see that he put the Agar-Agar on his Cream of Wheat. As if, Miss Willerton thought, after having done it for fifty years, he'd be capable of doing anything else. The breakfast dispute always started with Garner's Cream of Wheat and ended with her three spoonfuls of pineapple crush. "You know your acid, Willie," Miss Lucia would always say, "you know your acid"; and then Garner would roll his eyes and make some sickening remark and Bertha would jump and Lucia would look distressed and Miss Willerton would taste the pineapple crush she had already swallowed.

It was a relief to crumb the table. Crumbing the table gave one time to think, and if Miss Willerton were going to write a story, she had to think about it first. She could usually think best sitting in front of her typewriter, but this would do for the time being. First, she had to think of a subject to write a story about. There were so many subjects to write stories about that Miss Willerton never could think of one. That was always the hardest part of writing a story, she always said. She spent more time thinking of something to write about than she did writing. Sometimes she discarded subject after subject and it usually took her a week or two to decide finally on something. Miss Willerton got out the silver crumber and the crumb-catcher and started stroking the table. I wonder, she mused, if a baker would make a good subject? Foreign bakers were very picturesque, she thought. Aunt Myrtile Filmer had left her four color-tints of French bakers in mushroom-looking hats. They were great tall fellows—blond and. . . .

"Willie!" Miss Lucia screamed, entering the dining room with the saltcellars. "For heaven's sake, hold the catcher under the crumber or you'll have those crumbs on the rug. I've Bisseled it four times in the last week and I am not going to do it again."

"You have not Bisseled it on account of any crumbs I have spilled," Miss Willerton said tersely. "I always pick up the crumbs I drop," and she added, "I drop relatively few."

"And wash the crumber before you put it up this time," Miss Lucia returned.

Miss Willerton drained the crumbs into her hand and threw them out the window. She took the catcher and crumber to the kitchen and ran them under the cold-water faucet. She dried them and stuck them back in the drawer. That was over. Now she could get to the typewriter. She could stay there until dinnertime.

Miss Willerton sat down at her typewriter and let out her breath. Now! What had she been thinking about? Oh. Bakers. Hmmm. Bakers. No, bakers wouldn't do. Hardly colorful enough. No social tension connected with bakers. Miss Willerton sat staring through her typewriter. A S D F G—her eyes wandered over the keys. Hmmm. Teachers? Miss Willerton wondered. No. Heavens no. Teachers always made Miss Willerton feel peculiar. Her teachers at Willowpool Seminary had been all right but they were women. Willowpool Female Seminary, Miss Willerton remembered. She didn't like the phrase, Willowpool Female Seminary—it sounded biological. She always just said she was a graduate of Willowpool. Men teachers made Miss Willerton feel as if she were going to mispronounce something. Teachers weren't timely anyhow. They weren't even a social problem.

Social problem. Social problem. Hmmm. Sharecroppers! Miss Willerton had never been intimately connected with sharecroppers but, she reflected, they would make as arty a subject as any, and they would give her that air of social concern which was so valuable to have in the circles she was hoping to travel! "I can always capitalize," she muttered, "on the hookworm." It was coming to her now! Certainly! Her fingers plinked excitedly over the keys, never touching them. Then suddenly she began typing at great speed.

"Lot Motun," the typewriter registered, "called his dog." "Dog" was followed by an abrupt pause. Miss Willerton always did her best work on the first sentence. "First sentences," she always said, "came to her—like a flash! Just like a flash!" she would say and snap her fingers, "like a flash!" And she built her story up from them. "Lot Motun called his dog" had been automatic with Miss Willerton, and reading the sentence over, she decided that not only was "Lot Motun" a good name for a sharecropper, but also that having him call his dog was an excellent thing to have a sharecropper do. "The dog pricked up its ears and slunk over to Lot." Miss Willerton had the sentence down before she realized her error—two "Lots" in one paragraph. That was displeasing to the ear. The typewriter grated back and Miss Willerton applied three x's to "Lot." Over it she wrote in pencil, "him." Now she was ready to go again. "Lot Motun called his dog. The dog pricked up its ears and slunk over to him." Two dogs, too, Miss Willerton thought. Ummm. But that didn't affect the ears like two "Lots," she decided.

Miss Willerton was a great believer in what she called "phonetic art." She maintained that the ear was as much a reader as the eye. She liked to express it that way. "The eye forms a picture," she had told a group at the United Daughters of the Colonies, "that can be painted in the abstract, and the success of a literary venture" (Miss Willerton liked thc phrase, 'literary venture') "depends on the abstract created in the mind and the tonal quality" (Miss Willerton also liked 'tonal quality') "registered in the ear." There was something biting and sharp about "Lot Motun called his dog"; followed by "the dog pricked up its ears and slunk over to him," it gave the paragraph just the send-off it needed.

"He pulled the animal's short, scraggy ears and rolled over with it in the mud." Perhaps, Miss Willerton mused, that would be overdoing it. But a sharecropper, she knew, might reasonably be expected to roll over in the mud. Once she had read a novel dealing with that kind of people in which they had done just as bad and, throughout three-fourths of the narrative, much worse. Lucia found it in cleaning out one of Miss Willerton's bureau drawers and after glancing at a few random pages took it between thumb and index finger to the furnace and threw it in. "When I was cleaning your bureau out this morning, Willie, I found a book that Garner must have put there for a joke," Miss Lucia told her later. "It was awful, but you know how Garner is. I burned it." And then, tittering, she added, "I was sure it couldn't be yours." Miss Willerton was sure it could be none other's than hers but she hesitated in claiming the distinction. She had ordered it from the publisher because she didn't want to ask for it at the library. It had cost her $3.75 with the postage and she had not finished the last four chapters. At least, she had got enough from it, though, to be able to say that Lot Motun might reasonably roll over in the mud with his dog. Having him do that would give more point to the hookworm, too, she decided. "Lot Motun called his dog. The dog pricked up its ears and slunk over to him. He pulled the animal's short, scraggy ears and rolled over with it in the mud."

Miss Willerton settled back. That was a good beginning. Now she would plan her action. There had to be a woman, of course. Perhaps Lot could kill her. That type of woman always started trouble. She might even goad him on to kill her because of her wantonness and then he would be pursued by his conscience maybe.

He would have to have principles if that were going to be the case, but it would be fairly easy to give him those. Now how was she going to work that in with all the love interest there'd have to be, she wondered. There would have to be some quite violent, naturalistic scenes, the sadistic sort of thing one read of in connection with that class. It was a problem. However, Miss Willerton enjoyed such problems. She liked to plan passionate scenes best of all, but when she came to write them, she always began to feel peculiar and to wonder what the family would say when they read them. Garner would snap his fingers and wink at her at every opportunity; Bertha would think she was terrible; and Lucia would say in that silly voice of hers, "What have you been keeping from us, Willie? What have you been keeping from us?" and titter like she always did. But Miss Willerton couldn't think about that now; she had to plan her characters.

Lot would be tall, stooped, and shaggy but with sad eyes that made him look like a gentleman in spite of his red neck and big fumbling hands. He'd have straight teeth and, to indicate that he had some spirit, red hair. His clothes would hang on him but he'd wear them nonchalantly like they were part of his skin; maybe, she mused, he'd better not roll over with the dog after all. The woman would be more or less pretty—yellow hair, fat ankles, muddy-colored eyes.

She would get supper for him in the cabin and he'd sit there eating the lumpy grits she hadn't bothered to put salt in and thinking about something big, something way off—another cow, a painted house, a clean well, a farm of his own even. The woman would yowl at him for not cutting enough wood for her stove and would whine about the pain in her back. She'd sit and stare at him eating the sour grits and say he didn't have nerve enough to steal food. "You're just a damn beggar!" she'd sneer. Then he'd tell her to keep quiet. "Shut your mouth!" he'd shout. "I've taken all I'm gonna." She'd roll her eyes, mocking him, and laugh—"I ain't afraid er nothin' that looks like you." Then he'd push his chair behind him and head toward her. She'd snatch a knife off the table—Miss Willerton wondered what kind of a fool the woman was—and back away holding it in front of her. He'd lunge forward but she'd dart from him like a wild horse. Then they'd face each other again—their eyes brimming with hate— and sway back and forth. Miss Willerton could hear the seconds dropping on the tin roof outside. He'd dart at her again but she'd have the knife ready and would plunge it into him in an instant—Miss Willerton could stand it no longer. She struck the woman a terrific blow on the head from behind. The knife dropped out of her hands and a mist swept her from the room. Miss Willerton turned to Lot. "Let me get you some hot grits," she said. She went over to the stove and got a clean plate of smooth white grits and a piece of butter.

"Gee, thanks," Lot said and smiled at her with his nice teeth. "You always fix 'em just right. You know," he said, "I been thinkin'—we could get out of this tenant farm. We could have a decent place. If we made anything this year over, we could put it in a cow an' start buildin' things up. Think what it would mean, Willie, just think."

She sat down beside him and put her hand on his shoulder. "We'll do it," she said. "We'll make better than we've made any year and by spring we should have us that cow."

"You always know how I feel, Willie," he said. "You always have known."

They sat there for a long time thinking of how well they understood each other. "Finish your food," she said finally.

After he had eaten, he helped her take the ashes out the stove and then, in the hot July evening, they walked down the pasture toward the creek and talked about the place they were going to have some day.

When late March came and the rainy season was almost there, they had accomplished almost more than was believable. For the past month, Lot had been up every morning at five, and Willy an hour earlier to get in all the work they could while the weather was clear. Next week, Lot said, the rain would probably start and if they didn't get the crop in by then, they would lose it—and all they had gained in the past months. They knew what that meant—another year of getting along with no more than they'd had the last. Then too, there'd be a baby next year instead of a cow. Lot had wanted the cow anyway. "Children don't cost all that much to feed," he'd argued, "an' the cow would help feed him," but Willie had been firm—the cow could come later— the child must have a good start. "Maybe," Lot had said finally, "we'll have enough for both," and he had gone out to look at the new-plowed ground as if he could count the harvest from the furrows.

Even with as little as they'd had, it had been a good year. Willie had cleaned the shack, and Lot had fixed the chimney. There was a profusion of petunias by the doorstep and a colony of snapdragons under the window. It had been a peaceful year. But now they were becoming anxious over the crop. They must gather it before the rain. "We need another week," Lot muttered when he came in that night. "One more week an' we can do it. Do you feel like gatherin'? It isn't right that you should have to," he sighed, "but I can't hire any help."

"I'm all right," she said, hiding her trembling hands behind her. "I'll gather."

"It's cloudy tonight," Lot said darkly.

The next day they worked until nightfall—worked until they could work no longer and then stumbled back to the cabin and fell into bed.

Willie woke in the night conscious of a pain. It was a soft, green pain with purple lights running through it. She wondered if she were awake. Her head rolled from side to side and there were droning shapes grinding boulders in it.

Lot sat up. "Are you bad off?" he asked, trembling.

She raised herself on her elbow and then sank down again. "Get Anna up by the creek," she gasped.

The droning became louder and the shapes grayer. The pain intermingled with them for seconds first, then interminably. It came again and again. The sound of the droning grew more distinct and toward morning she realized that it was rain. Later she asked hoarsely, "How long has it been raining?"

"Most two days, now," Lot answered.

"Then we lost." Willie looked listlessly out at the dripping trees. "It's over."

"It isn't over," he said softly. "We got a daughter."

"You wanted a son."

"No, I got what I wanted—two Willies instead of one—that's better than a cow, even," he grinned. "What can I do to deserve all I got, Willie?" He bent over and kissed her forehead.

"What can I?" she asked slowly. "And what can I do to help you more?"

"How about your going to the grocery, Willie?"

Miss Willerton shoved Lot away from her. "W-what did you say, Lucia?" she stuttered.

"I said how about your going to the grocery this time? I've been every morning this week and I'm busy now."

Miss Willerton pushed back from the typewriter. "Very well," she said sharply. "What do you want there?"

"A dozen eggs and two pounds of tomatoes—ripe tomatoes—and you'd better start doctoring that cold right now. Your eyes are already watering and you're hoarse. There's Empirin in the bathroom. Write a check on the house for the groceries. And wear your coat. It's cold."

Miss Willerton rolled her eyes upward. "I am forty-four years old," she announced, "and able to take care of myself."

"And get ripe tomatoes," Miss Lucia returned.

Miss Willerton, her coat buttoned unevenly, tramped up Broad Street and into the supermarket. "What was it now?" she muttered. "Two dozen eggs and a pound of tomatoes, yes." She passed the lines of canned vegetables and the crackers and headed for the box where the eggs were kept. But there were no eggs. "Where are the eggs?" she asked a boy weighing snap-beans.

"We ain't got nothin' but pullet eggs," he said, fishing up another handful of beans.

"Well, where are they and what is the difference?" Miss Willerton demanded.

He threw several beans back into the bin, slouched over to the egg box and handed her a carton. "There ain't no difference really," he said, pushing his gum over his front teeth. "A teen-age chicken or somethin', I don't know. You want 'em?"

"Yes, and two pounds of tomatoes. Ripe tomatoes," Miss Willerton added. She did not like to do the shopping. There was no reason those clerks should be so condescending. That boy wouldn't have dawdled with Lucia. She paid for the eggs and tomatoes and left hurriedly. The place depressed her somehow.

Silly that a grocery should depress one—nothing in it but trifling domestic doings—women buying beans—riding children in those grocery go-carts—higgling about an eighth of a pound more or less of squash—what did they get out of it? Miss Willerton wondered. Where was there any chance for self-expression, for creation, for art? All around her it was the same—sidewalks full of people scurrying about with their hands full of little packages and their minds full of little packages—that woman there with the child on the leash, pulling him, jerking him, dragging him away from a window with a jack-o'-lantern in it; she would probably be pulling and jerking him the rest of her life. And there was another, dropping a shopping bag all over the street, and another wiping a child's nose, and up the street an old woman was coming with three grandchildren jumping all over her, and behind them was a couple walking too close for refinement.

Miss Willerton looked at the couple sharply as they came nearer and passed. The woman was plump with yellow hair and fat ankles and muddy-colored eyes. She had on high-heel pumps and blue anklets, a too-short cotton dress, and a plaid jacket. Her skin was mottled and her neck thrust forward as if she were sticking it out to smell something that was always being drawn away. Her face was set in an inane grin. The man was long and wasted and shaggy. His shoulders were stooped and there were yellow knots along the side of his large, red neck. His hands fumbled stupidly with the girl's as they slumped along, and once or twice he smiled sickly at her and Miss Willerton could see that he had straight teeth and sad eyes and a rash over his forehead.

"Ugh," she shuddered.

Miss Willerton laid the groceries on the kitchen table and went back to her typewriter. She looked at the paper in it. "Lot Motun called his dog," it read. "The dog pricked up its ears and slunk over to him. He pulled the animal's short, scraggy ears and rolled over with it in the mud."

"That sounds awful!" Miss Willerton muttered. "It's not a good subject anyway," she decided. She needed something more colorful—more arty. Miss Willerton looked at her type-writer for a long time. Then of a sudden her fist hit the desk in several ecstatic little bounces. "The Irish!" she squealed. "The Irish!" Miss Willerton had always admired the Irish. Their brogue, she thought, was full of music; and their history—splendid! And the people, she mused, the Irish people! They were full of spirit—red-haired, with broad shoulders and great, drooping mustaches.

Enoch and the Gorilla

Flannery O'Connor

ENOCH Emery had borrowed his landlady's umbrella and he discovered as he stood in the entrance of the drugstore, trying to open it, that it was at least as old as she was. When he finally got it hoisted, he pushed his dark glasses back on his eyes and re-entered the downpour.

The umbrella was one his landlady had stopped using fifteen years before (which was the only reason she had lent it to him) and as soon as the rain touched the top of it, it came down with a shriek and stabbed him in the back of the neck. He ran a few feet with it over his head and then backed into another store entrance and removed it. Then to get it up again, he had to place the tip of it on the ground and ram it open with his foot. He ran out again, holding his hand up near the spokes to keep them open and this allowed the handle, which was carved to represent the head of a fox terrier, to jab him every few seconds in the stomach. He proceeded for another quarter of a block this way before the back half of the silk stood up off the spokes and allowed the storm to sweep down his collar. Then he ducked under the marquee of a movie house. It was Saturday and there were a lot of children standing more or less in a line in front of the ticket box.

Enoch was not very fond of children, but children always seemed to like to look at him. The line turned and twenty or thirty eyes began to observe him with a steady interest. The umbrella had assumed an ugly position, half up and half down, and the half that was up was about to come down and spill more water under his collar. When this happened the children laughed and jumped up and down. Enoch glared at them and turned his back and lowered his dark glasses. He found himself facing a life-size four-color picture of a gorilla. Over the gorilla's head, written in red letters was "GONGA! Giant Jungle Monarch and a Great Star! HERE IN PERSON!!!" At the level of the gorilla's knee, there was more that said, "Gonga will appear in person in front of this theater at 12 A.M. *TODAY!* A free pass to the first ten brave enough to step up and shake his hand!"

Enoch was usually thinking of something else at the moment that Fate began drawing back her leg to kick him. When he was four years old, his father had brought him home a tin box from the penitentiary. It was orange and had a picture of some peanut brittle on the outside of it and green letters that said, "A NUTTY SURPRISE!" When Enoch had opened it, a coiled piece of steel had sprung out at him and broken off the ends of his two front teeth. His life was full of so many happenings like that that it would seem he should have been more sensitive to his times of danger. He stood there and read the poster twice through carefully. To his mind, an opportunity to insult a successful ape came from the hand of Providence.

He turned around and asked the nearest child what time it was. The child said it was twelve-ten and that Gonga was already ten minutes late. Another child said that maybe the rain had delayed him. Another said, no not the rain, his director was taking a plane from Hollywood. Enoch gritted his teeth. The first child said that if he wanted to shake the star's hand, he would have to get in line like the rest of them and wait his turn. Enoch got in line. A child asked him how old he was. Another observed that he had funny-looking teeth. He ignored all this as best he could and began to straighten out the umbrella.

In a few minutes a black truck turned around the corner and came slowly up the street in the heavy rain. Enoch pushed the umbrella under his arm and began to squint through his dark glasses. As the truck approached, a phonograph inside it began to play "Tarara Boom Di Aye," but the music was almost drowned out by the rain. There was a large illustration of a blonde on the outside of the truck, advertising some picture other than the gorilla's.

The children held their line carefully as the truck stopped in front of the movie house. The back door of it was constructed like a paddy wagon, with a grate, but the ape was not at it. Two men in raincoats got out of the cab part, cursing, and ran around to the back and opened the door. One of them stuck his head in and said, "Okay, make it snappy, willya?" The other jerked his thumb at the children and said, "Get back willya, willya get back?"

A voice on the record inside the truck said, "Here's Gonga, folks, Roaring Gonga and a Great Star! Give Gonga a big hand, folks!" The voice was barely a mumble in the rain.

The man who was waiting by the door of the truck stuck his head in again. "Okay willya get out?" he said.

There was a faint thump somewhere inside the van. After a second a dark furry arm emerged just enough for the rain to touch it and then drew back inside.

"Goddamn," the man who was under the marquee said; he took off his raincoat and threw it to the man by the door, who threw it into the wagon. After two or three minutes more, the gorilla appeared at the door, with the raincoat buttoned up to his chin and the collar turned up. There was an iron chain hanging from around his neck; the man grabbed it and pulled him down and the two of them bounded under the marquee together. A motherly-looking woman was in the glass ticket box, getting the passes ready for the first ten children brave enough to step up and shake hands.

The gorilla ignored the children entirely and followed the man over to the other side of the entrance where there was a small platform raised about a foot off the ground. He stepped up on it and turned facing the children and began to growl. His growls were not so much loud as poisonous; they appeared to issue from a black heart. Enoch was terrified and if he had not been surrounded by the children, he would have run away.

"Who'll step up first?" the man said. "Come on come on, who'll step up first? A free pass to the first kid stepping up."

There was no movement from the group of children. The man glared at them. "What's the matter with you kids?" he barked. "You yellow? He won't hurt you as long as I got him by this chain." He tightened his grip on the chain and jangled it at them to show he was holding it securely.

After a minute a little girl separated herself from the group. She had long wood-shaving curls and a fierce triangular face. She moved up to within four feet of the star.

"Okay okay," the man said, rattling the chain, "make it snappy."

The ape reached out and gave her hand a quick shake. By this time there was another little girl ready and then two boys. The line re-formed and began to move up.

The gorilla kept his hand extended and turned his head away with a bored look at the rain. Enoch had got over his fear and was trying frantically to think of an obscene remark that would be suitable to insult him with. Usually he didn't have any trouble with this kind of composition but nothing came to him now.

His brain, both parts, was completely empty. He couldn't think even of the insulting phrases he used every day.

There were only two children in front of him by now. The first one shook hands and stepped aside. Enoch's heart was beating violently. The children in front of him finished and stepped aside and left him facing the ape, who took his hand with an automatic motion.

It was the first hand that had been extended to Enoch since he had come to the city. It was warm and soft.

For a second he only stood there, clasping it. Then he began to stammer. "My name is Enoch Emery," he mumbled. "I attended the Rodemill Boys' Bible Academy. I work at the city zoo. I seen two of your pictures. I'm only eighteen years old but I already work for the city. My daddy made me come . . ." and his voice cracked.

The star leaned slightly forward and a change came in his eyes: an ugly pair of human ones moved closer and squinted at Enoch from behind the celluloid pair. "You go to hell," a surly voice inside the ape-suit said, low but distinctly, and the hand was jerked away.

Enoch's humiliation was so sharp and painful that he turned around three times before he realized which direction he wanted to go in. Then he ran off into the rain as fast as he could.

In spite of himself, Enoch couldn't get over the expectation that something was going to happen to him. The virtue of hope, in Enoch, was made up of two parts suspicion and one part lust. It operated on him all the rest of the day. He had only a vague idea what he wanted, but he was not a boy without ambition: he wanted to become something. He wanted to better his condition. He wanted, some day, to see a line of people waiting to shake his hand.

All afternoon he fidgeted and fooled in his room, biting his nails and shredding what was left of the silk off the landlady's umbrella. Finally he denuded it entirely and broke off the spokes. What was left was a black stick with a sharp steel point at one end and a dog's head at the other. It might have been an instrument for some specialized kind of torture that had gone out of fashion. Enoch walked up and down his room with it under his arm and realized that it would distinguish him on the sidewalk.

About seven o'clock in the evening he put on his coat and took the stick and headed for a little restaurant two blocks away. He had the sense that he was setting off to get some honor, but he was very nervous, as if he were afraid he might have to snatch it instead of receive it.

He never set out for anything without eating first. The restaurant was called the Paris Diner; it was a tunnel about six feet wide, located between a shoeshine parlor and a dry-cleaning establishment. Enoch slid in and climbed up on the far stool at the counter and said he would have a bowl of split-pea soup and a chocolate malted milkshake.

The waitress was a tall woman with a big yellow dental plate and the same color hair done up in a black hairnet. One hand never left her hip; she filled orders with the other one. Although Enoch came in every night, she had never learned to like him.

Instead of filling his order, she began to fry bacon; there was only one other customer in the place and he had finished his meal and was reading a newspaper; there was no one to eat the bacon but her. Enoch reached over the counter and prodded her hip with the stick. "Listenhere," he said, "I got to go. I'm in a hurry."

"Go then," she said. Her jaw began to work and she stared into the skillet with a fixed attention.

"Lemme just have a piece of theter cake yonder," he said, pointing to a half of pink and yellow cake on a round glass stand. "I think I got something to do. I got to be going. Set it up there next to him," he said, indicating the customer reading the newspaper. He slid over the stools and began reading the outside sheet of the man's paper.

The man lowered the paper and looked at him. Enoch smiled. The man raised the paper again. "Could I borrow some part of your paper that you ain't studying?" Enoch asked. The man lowered it again and stared at him; he had muddy unflinching eyes. He leafed deliberately through the paper and shook out the sheet with the comic strips and handed it to Enoch. It was Enoch's favorite part. He read it every evening like an office. While he ate the cake that the waitress had torpedoed down the counter at him, he read and felt himself surge with kindness and courage and strength.

When he finished one side, he turned the sheet over and began to scan the advertisements for movies that filled the other side. His eye went over three columns without stopping; then it came to a box that advertised Gonga, Giant Jungle Monarch, and listed the theaters he would visit on his tour and the hours he would be at each one. In thirty minutes he would arrive at the Victory on 57th Street and that would be his last appearance in the city.

If anyone had watched Enoch read this, he would have seen a certain transformation in his countenance. It still shone with the inspiration he had absorbed from the comic strips, but something else had come over it: a look of awakening.

The waitress happened to turn around to see if he hadn't gone. "What's the matter with you?" she said. "Did you swallow a seed?"

"I know what I want," Enoch murmured.

"I know what I want too," she said with a dark look.

Enoch felt for his stick and laid his change on the counter. "I got to be going."

"Don't let me keep you," she said.

"You may not see me again," he said, "—the way I am."

"Any way I don't see you will be all right with me," she said.

Enoch left. It was a pleasant damp evening. The puddles on the sidewalk shone and the store windows were steamy and bright with junk. He disappeared down a side street and made his way rapidly along the darker passages of the city, pausing only once or twice at the end of an alley to dart a glance in each direction before he ran on. The Victory was a small theater, suited to the needs of the family, in one of the closer subdivisions; he passed through a succession of lighted areas and then on through more alleys and back streets until he came to the business section that surrounded it. Then he slowed up. He saw it about a block away, glittering in its darker setting. He didn't cross the street to the side it was on but kept on the far side, moving forward with his squint fixed on the glary spot. He stopped when he was directly across from it and hid himself in a narrow stair cavity that divided a building.

The truck that carried Gonga was parked across the street and the star was standing under the marquee, shaking hands with an elderly woman. She moved aside and a gentleman in a polo shirt stepped up and shook hands vigorously, like a sportsman. He was followed by a boy of about three who wore a tall Western hat that nearly covered his face; he had to be pushed ahead by the line. Enoch watched for some time, his face working with envy. The small boy was followed by a lady in shorts, she by an old man who tried to draw extra attention to himself by dancing up instead of walking in a dignified way. Enoch suddenly darted across the street and slipped noiselessly into the open back door of the truck.

The handshaking went on until the feature picture was ready to begin. Then the star got back in the van and the people filed into the theater. The driver and the man who was master of ceremonies climbed in the cab part and the truck rumbled off. It crossed the city rapidly and continued on the highway, going very fast.

There came from the van certain thumping noises, not those of the normal gorilla, but they were drowned out by the drone of the motor and the steady sound of wheels against the road. The night was pale and quiet, with nothing to stir it but an occasional complaint from a hoot owl and the distant muted jarring of a freight train. The truck sped on until it slowed for a crossing, and as the van rattled over the tracks, a figure slipped from the door and almost fell, and then limped hurriedly off toward the woods.

Once in the darkness of a pine thicket, he laid down a pointed stick he had been clutching and something bulky and loose that he had been carrying under his arm, and began to undress. He folded each garment neatly after he had taken it off and then stacked it on top of the last thing he had removed. When all his clothes were in the pile, he took up the stick and began making a hole in the ground with it.

The darkness of the pine grove was broken by paler moonlit spots that moved over him now and again and showed him to be Enoch. His natural appearance was marred by a gash that ran from the corner of his lip to his collarbone and by a lump under his eye that gave him a dulled insensitive look. Nothing could have been more deceptive for he was burning with the intensest kind of happiness.

He dug rapidly until he had made a trench about a foot long and a foot deep. Then he placed the stack of clothes in it and stood aside to rest a second. Burying his clothes was not a symbol to him of burying his former self; he only knew he wouldn't need them any more. As soon as he got his breath, he pushed the displaced dirt over the hole and stamped it down with his foot. He discovered while he did this that he still had his shoes on, and when he finished, he removed them and threw them from him. Then he picked up the loose bulky object and shook it vigorously.

In the uncertain light, one of his lean white legs could be seen to disappear and then the other, one arm and then the other: a black heavier shaggier figure replaced his. For an instant, it had two heads, one light and one dark, but after a second, it pulled the dark black head over the other and corrected this. It busied itself with certain hidden fastenings and what appeared to be minor adjustments of its hide.

For a time after this, it stood very still and didn't do anything. Then it began to growl and beat its chest; it jumped up and down and flung its arms and thrust its head forward. The growls were thin and uncertain at first but they grew louder after a second. They became low and poisonous, louder again, low and poisonous again; they stopped altogether. The figure extended its hand, clutched nothing, and shook its arm vigorously; it withdrew the arm, extended it again, clutched nothing, and shook. It repeated this four or five times. Then it picked up the pointed stick and placed it at a cocky angle under its arm and left the woods for the highway. No gorilla anywhere, Africa or California or New York, was happier than he.

A man and woman sitting close together on a rock just off the highway were looking across an open stretch of valley at a view of the city in the distance and they didn't see the shaggy figure approaching. The smokestacks and square tops of buildings made a black uneven wall against the lighter sky and here and there a steeple cut a sharp wedge out of a cloud. The young man turned his neck just in time to see the gorilla standing a few feet away, hideous and black, with its hand extended. He eased his arm from around the woman and disappeared silently into the woods. She, as soon as she turned her eyes, fled screaming down the highway. The gorilla stood as though surprised and presently its arm fell to its side. It sat down on the rock where they had been sitting and stared over the valley at the uneven skyline of the city.

The Rain Guitar

James Dickey

—England, 1962—

The water-grass under had never waved
But one way. It showed me that flow is forever
Sealed from rain in a weir. For some reason having
To do with Winchester, I was sitting on my guitar case
Watching nothing but eelgrass trying to go downstream with all
the right motions
But one. I had on a sweater, and my threads were opening
Like mouths with rain. It mattered to me not at all
That a bridge was stumping
With a man, or that he came near and cast a fish
thread into the weir. I had no line and no feeling.
I had nothing to do with fish
But my eyes on the grass they hid in, waving with the one move
of trying
To be somewhere else. With what I had, what could I do?
I got out my guitar, that somebody told me was supposed to
improve
With moisture—or was it when it dried out?—and hit the lowest
And loudest chord. The drops that were falling just then
Hammered like Georgia railroad track
With E. The man went into a kind of fishing
Turn. Play it, he said through his pipe. There
I went, fast as I could with cold fingers. The strings shook
With drops. A buck dance settled on the weir. Where was the
city
Cathedral in all this? Out of sight, but somewhere around.
Play a little more
Of that, he said, and cast. Music-wood shone,
Getting worse or better faster than it liked:
Improvement or disintegration
Supposed to take years, fell on it
By the gallon. It darkened and rang

Like chimes. My sweater collapsed, and the rain reached
My underwear. I picked, the guitar showered, and he cast to the
mountain
Music. His wood leg tapped
On the cobbles. Memories of many men
Hung, rain-faced, improving, sealed-off
In the weir. I found myself playing Australian
Versions of British marching songs. Mouths opened all over me;
I sang,
His legs beat and marched
Like companions. I was Air Force,
I said. So was I; I picked
This up in Burma, he said, tapping his gone leg
With his fly rod, as Burma and the South
west Pacific and North Georgia reeled,
Rapped, cast, chimed, darkened and drew down
Cathedral water, and improved.

Sled Burial, Dream Ceremony

James Dickey

While the south rains, the north
Is snowing, and the dead southerner
Is taken there. He lies with the top of his casket
Open, his hair combed, the particles in the air
Changing to other things. The train stops

In a small furry village, and men in flap-eared caps
And others with women's scarves tied around their heads
And business hats over those, unload him,
And one of them reaches inside the coffin and places
The southerner's hand at the center

Of his dead breast. They load him onto a sled,
An old-fashioned sled with high-curled runners,
Drawn by horses with bells, and begin
To walk out of town, past dull red barns
Inching closer to the road as it snows

Harder, past an army of gunny-sacked bushes,
Past horses with flakes in the hollows of their sway-backs,
Past round faces drawn by children
On kitchen windows, all shedding basic-shaped tears.
The coffin top still is wide open;

His dead eyes stare through his lids,
Not fooled that the snow is cotton. The woods fall
Slowly off all of them, until they are walking
Between rigid little houses of ice-fishers
On a plain which is a great plain of water

Until the last rabbit track fails, and they are
At the center. They take axes, shovels, mattocks,
Dig the snow away, and saw the ice in the form
Of his coffin, lifting the slab like a door
Without hinges. The snow creaks under the sled

As they unload him like hay, holding his weight by ropes.
Sensing an unwanted freedom, a fish
Slides by, under the hole leading up through the snow
To nothing, and is gone. The coffin's shadow
Is white, and they stand there, gunny-sacked bushes,

Summoned from village sleep into someone else's dream
Of death, and let him down, still seeing the flakes in the air
At the place they are born of pure shadow
Like his dead eyelids, rocking for a moment like a boat
On utter foreignness, before he fills and sails down.

That Distant Land

Wendell Berry

FOR several days after the onset of his decline, my grandfather's mind seemed to leave him to go wandering, lost, in some foreign place. It was a dream he was in, we thought, that he could not escape. He was looking for the way home, and he could not find anyone who knew how to get there.

"No," he would say. "Port William. Port William is the name of the place."

Or he would ask, "Would you happen to know a nice lady by the name of Margaret Feltner? She lives in Port William. Now, which way would I take to get there?"

But it was not us he was asking. He was not looking at us and mistaking us for other people. He was not looking at us at all. He was talking to people he was meeting in his dream. From the way he spoke to them, they seemed to be nice people. They treated him politely and were kind, but they did not know any of the things that he knew, and they could not help him.

When his mind returned, it did so quietly. It had never been a mind that made a lot of commotion around itself. One morning when my grandmother went in to wake him and he opened his eyes, they were looking again. He looked at my grandmother and said, "Margaret, I'll declare." He looked around him at the bright room and out the window at the ridges and the woods, and said, "You got a nice place here, ma'am."

My grandmother, as joyful as if he had indeed been gone far away and had come home, said, "Oh, Mat, are you all right?"

And he said, "I seem to be a man who has been all right before, and I'm all right now."

That was the middle of June, and having come back from wherever it had been, his mind stayed with him and with us, a peaceable, pleasant guest, until he died.

He did not get out of bed again. What troubled us, and then grieved us, and finally consoled us, was that he made no effort to get up. It appeared to us that he felt his time of struggle to be past, and that he agreed to its end. He who had lived by ceaseless effort now lived simply as his life was given to him, day by day. During the time his mind had wandered he ate little or nothing, and though his mind returned his appetite did not. He ate to please my grandmother, but he could not eat much. She would offer the food, he would eat the few bites that were enough, and she would take the plate away. None of us had the heart to go beyond her gentle offering. No one insisted. No one begged. He asked almost nothing of us, only to be there with us, and we asked only to be with him.

He lay in a room on the east side of the house, so that from the window he could look out across the ridges toward the river valley. And he did often lie there looking out. Now that he felt his own claims removed from it, the place seemed to have become more than ever interesting to him, and he watched it as the dark lifted from it and the sun rose and moved above it and set and the dark returned. Now and then he would speak of what he saw—the valley brimming with fog in the early morning, a hawk circling high over the ridges, somebody at work in one of the fields—and we would know that he watched with understanding and affection. But the character of his watching had changed. We all felt it. We had known him as a man who watched, but then his watching had been purposeful. He had watched as a man preparing for what he knew he must do, and what he wanted to do. Now it had become the watching, almost, of one who was absent.

The room was bright in the mornings, and in the afternoons dim and cool. It was always clean and orderly. My grandfather, who had no wants, made no clutter around him, and any clutter that the rest of us made did not last long. His room became the center of the house, where we came to rest. He would welcome us, raising his hand to us as we came in, listening to all that was said, now and again saying something himself.

Because, wherever we were, we kept him in our minds, he kept us together in the world as we knew he kept us in his mind. Until the night of his death we were never all in the house at the same time, yet no day passed that he did not see most of us. In the morning, my mother, his only surviving child, or Hannah Coulter, who had been his daughter-in-law and was, in all but blood, his daughter, or Flora, my wife, or Sara, my brother Henry's wife, would come in to spend the day with my grandmother to keep her company and help with the work. And at evening my father, or Henry, or I, or Nathan Coulter, who now farmed my grandfather's farm and was, in all but blood, his son, would come, turn about, to spend the night, to give whatever help would be needed.

And others who were not family came: Burley Coulter, Burley's brother Jarrat, Elton and Mary Penn, Arthur and Martin Rowanberry. They would happen by for a few minutes in the daytime, or come after supper and sit and talk an hour or two. We were a membership. We belonged together, and my grandfather's illness made us feel it.

But "illness," now that I have said it, seems the wrong word. It was not like other illnesses that I had seen—it was quieter and more peaceable. It was, it would be truer to say, a great weariness that had come upon him, like the lesser weariness that comes with the day's end—a weariness that had been earned, and was therefore accepted.

I had lived away, working in the city, for several years, and had returned home only that spring. I was thirty-one years old, I had a wife and children, and my return had given a sudden sharp clarity to my understanding of my home country. Every fold of the land, every grass blade and leaf of it gave me joy, for I saw how my own place in it had been prepared, along with its failures and its losses. Though I knew that I had returned to difficulties—not the least of which were the deaths that I could see coming—I was joyful.

The nights I spent, taking my turn, on the cot in a corner of my grandfather's room gave me a strong, sweet pleasure. At first, usually, visitors would be there, neighbors or family stopping by. Toward bedtime, they would go. I would sit on a while with my grandmother and grandfather, and we would talk. Or rather, if I could arrange it so, they would talk and I would listen. I loved to start them talking about old times—my mother's girlhood, their own young years, stories told them by their parents and grandparents, memories of memories. In their talk the history of Port William went back and back along one of its lineages until it ended in silence and conjecture, for Port William was older than its memories. That it had begun we knew because it had continued, but we did not know when or how it had begun.

It was usually easy enough to get them started, for they enjoyed the remembering, and they knew that I liked to hear.

"Grandad," I would say, "who was George Washington Coulter's mother?" Or: "Granny, tell about Aunt Maude Wheeler hailing the steamboat." And they would enter the endlessly varying pattern of remembering. A name would remind them of a story; one story would remind them of another. Sometimes my grandmother would get out a box of old photographs and we would sit close to the bed so that my grandfather could see them too, and then the memories and names moved and hovered over the transfixed old sights. The picture that most moved and troubled me was the only consciously photographed "scene": a look down the one street of Port William at the time of my grandparents' childhood—1890 or thereabouts. What so impressed me about it was that the town had then been both more prosperous and more the center of its own attention than I had ever known it to be. The business buildings all had upper stories, the church had a steeple, there was a row of trees, planted at regular intervals, along either side of the road. Now the steeple and most of the upper stories were gone—by wind or fire or decay—and many of the trees were gone. For a long time, in Port William, what had gone had not been replaced. Its own attention had turned away from itself toward what it could not be. And I understood how, in his dream, my grandfather had suffered his absence from the town; through much of his life it had grown increasingly absent from itself.

After a while, my grandmother would leave us. She would go to my grandfather's side and take his hand. "Mat, is there anything you want before I go?"

"Ma'am," he would say, "I've got everything I want." He would be teasing her a little, as he was always apt to do.

She would hesitate, wishing, I think, that he did want something. "Well, good night. I'll see you in the morning."

And he would pat her hand and say very agreeably, as if he were altogether willing for that to happen, if it should happen, "All right."

She would go and we would hear her stirring about in her room, preparing for bed. I would do everything necessary to make my grandfather comfortable for the night, help him to relieve himself, help him to turn onto his side, straighten the bedclothes, see that the flashlight was in reach in case he wanted to look at the clock, which he sometimes did. I was moved by his willingness to let me help him. We had always been collaborators. When I was little, he had been the one in the family who would help me with whatever I was trying to make. And now he accepted help as cheerfully as he had given it. We were partners yet.

I was still a young man, with a young man's prejudice in favor of young bodies. I would have been sorry but I would not have been surprised if I had found it unpleasant to have to handle him as I did—his old flesh slackened and dwindling on the bones—but I did not find it so. I touched him gratefully. I would put one knee on the bed and gather him in my arms and move him toward me and turn him. I liked to do it. The comfort I gave him I felt. He would say, "Thanks, son."

When he was settled, I would turn on the dim little bedlamp by the cot and go to bed myself.

"Sleep tight," I would tell him.

"Well," he would say, amused, "I will part of the time."

I would read a while, letting the remembered dear stillness of the old house come around me, and then I would sleep.

My grandfather did only sleep part of the time. Mostly, when he was awake, he lay quietly with his thoughts, but sometimes he would have to call me, and I would get up to bring him a drink (he would want only two or three swallows), or help him to use the bedpan, or help him to turn over.

Once he woke me to recite me the Twenty-third Psalm. "Andy," he said. "Andy. Listen." He said the psalm to me. I lay listening to his old, slow voice coming through the dark to me, saying that he walked through the valley of the shadow of death and that he feared no evil. It stood my hair up. I had known that psalm all my life. I had heard it and said it a thousand times. But until then I had always felt that it came from a long way off, some place I had not lived. Now, hearing him speak it, it seemed to me for the first time to utter itself in our tongue and to wear our dust. My grandfather slept again after that, but I did not.

Another night, again, I heard him call me. "Andy. Listen." His voice exultant then, at having recovered the words, he recited:

> There entertain him all the saints above,
> In solemn troops and sweet societies
> That sing, and singing in their glory move,
> And wipe the tears forever from his eyes.

After he spoke them, the words stood above us in the dark and the quiet, sounding and luminous. And then they faded.

After a while I said, "Who taught you that?"

"My mother. She was a great hand to improve your mind."

And after a while, again, I asked, "Do you know who wrote it?"

"No," he said. "But wasn't he a fine one!"

As the summer went along, he weakened, but so slowly we could hardly see it happening. There was never any sudden change. He remained quiet, mainly comfortable, and alert. We stayed in our routine of caring for him; it had become the ordinary way of things.

In the latter part of August we started into the tobacco cutting. For us, that is the great divider of the year. It ends the summer, and makes safe the season's growth. After it, our minds are lightened, and we look ahead to winter and the coming year. It is a sort of ritual of remembrance, too, when we speak of other years and remember our younger selves and the absent and the dead—all those we have, as we say, "gone down the row with."

We had a big crew that year—eight men working every day: Jarrat and Burley and Nathan Coulter, Arthur and Martin Rowanberry, Elton Penn, Danny Branch, and me. Hannah Coulter and Mary Penn and Lyda Branch kept us fed and helped with the hauling and housing. And Nathan's and Hannah's boy, Mattie, and the Penns' children, Elsie and Jack, were with us until school started, and then they worked after school and on Saturdays. We worked back and forth among the various farms as the successive plantings became ready for harvest.

"What every tobacco cutting needs," Art Rowanberry said, "is a bunch of eighteen-year-old boys wanting to show how fast they are."

He was right, but we did not have them. We were not living in a time that was going to furnish many such boys for such work. Except for Mattie and Jack, who were fourteen and eleven, and would have liked to show how fast they were, if they had been fast, we were all old enough to be resigned to the speed we could stand. And so, when we cut, we would be strung out along the field in a pattern that never varied from the first day to the last. First would be Elton and Nathan and Danny, all

working along together. Elton, I think, would have proved the
fastest if anybody had challenged him, but nobody did. Then
came Mart Rowanberry, who was always ahead of me, though
he was nearly twice my age, and then, some distance behind
me, would come Art Rowanberry, and then Burley Coulter, and
then, far back, Burley's brother Jarrat, whose judgment and
justification of himself were unswerving: "I'm old and wore out
and not worth a damn. But every row I cut is a cut row."

In my grandfather's absence Jarrat was the oldest of us, a
long-enduring, solitary, mostly silent man, slowed by age and
much hard work. His brushy eyes could stare upon you as if
you had no more ability to stare back than a post. When he had
something to say, his way was simply to begin to say it, no matter who else was talking or what else was happening, his slow,
hard-edged voice boring in upon us like his stare—and the result, invariably, was that whatever was happening stopped, and
whoever was talking listened.

I never caught up with Elton and Nathan and Danny, or came
anywhere near it, but at least when the rows were straight I always had them in sight, and I loved to watch them. Though they
kept an even, steady pace, it was not a slow one. They drove
into the work, maintaining the same pressing rhythm from one
end of the row to the other, and yet they worked well, as smooth-
ly and precisely as dancers. To see them moving side by side
against the standing crop, leaving it fallen, the field changed,
behind them, was maybe like watching Homeric soliders going
into battle. It was momentous and beautiful, and touchingly,
touchingly mortal. They were spending themselves as they
worked, giving up their time; they would not return by the way
they went.

The good crew men among us were Burley and Elton. When
the sun was hot and the going hard, it would put heart into us to
hear Burley singing out down the row some scrap of human sorrow that his flat, exuberant voice both expressed and mocked:

Allll our sins and griefs to bear-oh!

—that much only, raised abruptly out of the silence like the
howl of some solitary dog. Or he would sing with a lovelorn qua-
ver in his voice:

Darlin', fool yourself and love me one more time.

And when we were unloading the wagons in the barn, he would start his interminable tale about his life as a circus teamster. It was not meant to be believed, and yet in our misery we listened to his extravagant wonderful lies as if he had been Marco Polo returned from Cathay.

Elton had as much gab as Burley, when he wanted to, but he served us as the teller of the tale of our own work. He told and retold everything that happened that was funny. That we already knew what he was telling, that he was telling us what we ourselves had done, did not matter. He told it well, he told it the way we would tell it when we told it, and every time he told it he told it better. He told us, also, how much of our work we had got done, and how much we had left to do, and how we might form the tasks still ahead in order to do them. His head, of course, was not the only one involved, and not the only good one, but his was indeed a good one, and his use of it pleased him and comforted us. Though we had a lot of work still to do, we were going to be able to do it, and these were the ways we could get it done. The whole of it stayed in his mind. He shaped it for us and gave it a comeliness greater than its difficulty.

That we were together now kept us reminded of my grandfather, who had always been with us before. We often spoke of him, because we missed him, or because he belonged to our stories, and we could not tell them without speaking of him.

One morning, perhaps to acknowledge to herself that he would not wear them again, my grandmother gave me a pair of my grandfather's shoes.

It was a gift not easy to accept. I said, "Thanks, Granny," and put them under my arm.

"No," she said. "Put them on. See if they fit."

They fit, and I started, embarrassedly, to take them off.

"No," she said. "Wear them."

And so I wore them to the field.

"New shoes!" Burley said, recognizing them, and I saw tears start to his eyes.

"Yes," I said.

Burley studied them, and then me. And then he smiled and put his arm around me, making the truth plain and bearable to us both: "You can wear 'em, honey. But you can't fill 'em."

It got to be September, and the fall feeling came into the air. The days would get as hot as ever, but now when the sun got low the chill would come. It was not going to frost for a while yet, but we could feel it coming. It was the time of year, Elton said, when a man begins to remember his long underwear.

We were cutting a patch at Elton's place where the rows were longer than any we had cut before, bending around the shoulder of a ridge and rising a little over it. They were rows to break a man's heart, for, shaped as they were, you could not see the end, and those of us who were strung out behind the leaders could not see each other. All that we could see ahead of us would be the cloudless blue sky. Each row was a long, lonely journey that, somewhere in the middle, in our weariness, we believed would never end.

Once when I had cut my row and was walking back to start another, Art Rowanberry wiped the sweat from his nose on the cuff of his sleeve and called out cheerfully to me, "Well, have you been across? Have you seen the other side?"

That became the ceremony of that day and the next. When one of us younger ones finished a row and came walking back, Art would ask us, "Have you seen the other side?"

Burley would take it up then, mourning and mocking: "Have you reached the other shore, dear brother? Have you seen that distant land?" And he would sing,

Oh, pilgrim, have you seen that distant land?

On the evening of the second day we had the field nearly cut. There was just enough of the crop left standing to make an easy job of finishing up—something to look forward to. We had finished cutting for the day and were sitting in the rich, still light under a walnut tree at the edge of the field, resting a little, before loading the wagons. We would load them the last thing every evening, to unload the next morning while the dew was on.

We saw my father's car easing back along the fencerow, rocking a little over the rough spots in the ground. It was a gray car, all dusty, and scratched along the sides where he had driven it through the weeds and briars. He still had on his suit and tie.

"Ah, here he comes," Burley said, for we were used to seeing him at that time of day, when he would leave his office at Hargrave and drive up to help us a little or to see how we had got along.

He drove up beside us and stopped, and killed the engine. But he did not look at us. He looked straight ahead as if he had not quit driving, his hands still on the wheel.

"Boys," he said, "Mr. Feltner died this afternoon. About an hour ago."

And then, after he seemed to have finished, he said as though to himself, "And now that's over."

I heard Burley clear his throat, but nobody said anything. We sat in the cooling light in my grandfather's new silence, letting it come upon us.

And then the silence shifted and became our own. Nobody spoke. Nobody yet knew what to say. We did not know what we were going to do. We were, I finally realized, waiting on Jarrat. It was Elton's farm, but Jarrat was now the oldest man, and we were waiting on him.

He must have felt it too, for he stood, and stood still, looking at us, and then turned away from us toward the wagons.

"Let's load 'em up."

I've Been to the Mountaintop

Martin Luther King, Jr.

THANK you very kindly, my friends. As I listened to Ralph Abernathy in his eloquent and generous introduction and then thought about myself, I wondered who he was talking about. It's always good to have your closest friend and associate say something good about you. And Ralph is the best friend that I have in the world.

I'm delighted to see each of you here tonight in spite of a storm warning. You reveal that you are determined to go on anyhow. Something is happening in Memphis, something is happening in our world.

As you know, if I were standing at the beginning of time, with the possibility of general and panoramic view of the whole human history up to now, and the Almighty said to me, "Martin Luther King, which age would you like to live in?"—I would take my mental flight by Egypt through, or rather across the Red Sea, through the wilderness on toward the promised land. And in spite of its magnificence, I wouldn't stop there. I would move on by Greece, and take my mind to Mount Olympus. And I would see Plato, Aristotle, Socrates, Euripides and Aristophanes assembled around the Parthenon as they discussed the great and eternal issues of reality.

But I wouldn't stop there. I would go on, even to the great heyday of the Roman Empire. And I would see developments around there, through various emperors and leaders. But I wouldn't stop there. I would even come up to the day of the Renaissance, and get a quick picture of all that the Renaissance did for the cultural and esthetic life of man. But I wouldn't stop there. I would even go by the way that the man for whom I'm named had his habitat. And I would watch Martin Luther as he tacked his ninety-five theses on the door at the church in Wittenberg.

But I wouldn't stop there. I would come on up even to 1863, and watch a vacillating president by the name of Abraham Lincoln finally come to the conclusion that he had to sign the Emancipation Proclamation. But I wouldn't stop there. I would even come up to the early thirties, and see a man grappling with the problems of the bankruptcy of his nation. And come with an eloquent cry that we have nothing to fear but fear itself.

But I wouldn't stop there. Strangely enough, I would turn to the Almighty, and say, "If you allow me to live just a few years in the second half of the twentieth century, I will be happy." Now that's a strange statement to make, because the world is all messed up. The nation is sick. Trouble is in the land. Confusion all around. That's a strange statement. But I know, somehow, that only when it is dark enough, can you see the stars. And I see God working in this period of the twentieth century in a way that men, in some strange way, are responding—something is happening in our world. The masses of people are rising up. And wherever they are assembled today, whether they are in Johannesburg, South Africa; Nairobi, Kenya; Accra, Ghana; New York City; Atlanta, Georgia; Jackson, Mississippi; or Memphis, Tennessee—the cry is always the same—"We want to be free."

And another reason that I'm happy to live in this period is that we have been forced to a point where we're going to have to grapple with the problems that men have been trying to grapple with through history, but the demands didn't force them to do it. Survival demands that we grapple with them. Men, for years now, have been talking about war and peace. But now, no longer can they just talk about it. It is no longer a choice between violence and nonviolence in this world; it's nonviolence or nonexistence.

That is where we are today. And also in the human rights revolution, if something isn't done, and in a hurry, to bring the colored peoples of the world out of their long years of poverty, their long years of hurt and neglect, the whole world is doomed. Now, I'm just happy that God has allowed me to live in this period, to see what is unfolding. And I'm happy that he's allowed me to be in Memphis.

I can remember, I can remember when Negroes were just going around as Ralph has said, so often, scratching where they didn't itch, and laughing when they were not tickled. But that day is all over. We mean business now, and we are determined to gain our rightful place in God's world.

And that's all this whole thing is about. We aren't engaged in any negative protest and in any negative arguments with anybody. We are saying that we are determined to be men. We are determined to be people. We are saying that we are God's children. And that we don't have to live like we are forced to live.

Now, what does all of this mean in this great period of history? It means that we've got to stay together. We've got to stay together and maintain unity. You know, whenever Pharaoh wanted to prolong the period of slavery in Egypt, he had a favorite, favorite formula for doing it. What was that? He kept the slaves fighting among themselves. But whenever the slaves get together, something happens in Pharaoh's court, and he cannot hold the slaves in slavery. When the slaves get together, that's the beginning of getting out of slavery. Now let us maintain unity.

Secondly, let us keep the issues where they are. The issue is injustice. The issue is the refusal of Memphis to be fair and honest in its dealings with its public servants, who happen to be sanitation workers. Now, we've got to keep attention on that. That's always the problem with a little violence. You know what happened the other day, and the press dealt only with the window-breaking. I read the articles. They very seldom got around to mentioning the fact that one thousand, three hundred sanitation workers were on strike, and that Memphis is not being fair to them, and that Mayor Loeb is in dire need of a doctor. They didn't get around to that.

Now we're going to march again, and we've got to march again, in order to put the issue where it is supposed to be. And force everybody to see that there are thirteen hundred of God's children here suffering, sometimes going hungry, going through dark and dreary nights wondering how this thing is going to come out. That's the issue. And we've got to say to the nation: we know it's coming out. For when people get caught up with that which is right and they are willing to sacrifice for it, there is no stopping point short of victory.

We aren't going to let any mace stop us. We are masters in our nonviolent movement in disarming police forces; they don't know what to do. I've seen them so often. I remember in Birmingham, Alabama, when we were in that majestic struggle there we would move out of the 16th Street Baptist Church day after day; by the hundreds we would move out. And Bull Connor would tell them to send the dogs forth and they did come; but we just went before the dogs singing, "Ain't gonna let nobody turn me round." Bull Connor next would say, "Turn the fire hoses on." And as I said to you the other night, Bull Connor didn't know history. He knew a kind of physics that somehow didn't relate to the transphysics that we knew about. And that was the fact that there was a certain kind of fire that no water could put out. And we went before the fire hoses; we had known water. If we were Baptist or some other denomination, we had been immersed. If we were Methodist, and some others, we had been sprinkled, but we knew water.

That couldn't stop us. And we just went on before the dogs and we would look at them; and we'd go on before the water hoses and we would look at it, and we'd just go on singing "Over my head I see freedom in the air." And then we would be thrown in the paddy wagons, and sometimes we were stacked in there like sardines in a can. And they would throw us in, and old Bull would say, "Take them off," and they did; and we would just go in the paddy wagon singing, "We Shall Overcome." And every now and then we'd get in the jail, and we'd see the jailers looking through the windows being moved by our prayers, and being moved by our words and our songs. And there was a power there which Bull Connor couldn't adjust to; and so we ended up transforming Bull into a steer, and we won our struggle in Birmingham.

Now we've got to go on to Memphis just like that. I call upon you to be with us Monday. Now about injunctions: We have an injunction and we're going into court tomorrow morning to fight this illegal, unconstitutional injunction. All we say to America is, "Be true to what you said on paper." If I lived in China or even Russia, or any totalitarian country, maybe I could understand the denial of certain basic First Amendment privileges, because they hadn't committed themselves to that over there. But somewhere I read of the freedom of assembly. Somewhere I read of the freedom of speech. Somewhere I read of the freedom of the press. Somewhere I read that the greatness of America is the right to protest for right. And so just as I say, we aren't going to let any injunction turn us around. We are going on.

We need all of you. And you know what's beautiful to me, is to see all of these ministers of the Gospel. It's a marvelous picture. Who is it that is supposed to articulate the longings and aspirations of the people more than the preacher? Somehow the preacher must be an Amos, and say, "Let justice roll down like waters and righteousness like a mighty stream." Somehow, the preacher must say with Jesus, "The spirit of the Lord is upon me, because he hath anointed me to deal with the problems of the poor."

And I want to commend the preachers, under the leadership of these noble men: James Lawson, one who has been in this struggle for many years; he's been to jail for struggling; but he's still going on, fighting for the rights of his people. Rev. Ralph Jackson, Billy Kiles; I could just go right on down the list, but time will not permit. But I want to thank them all. And I want you to thank them, because so often, preachers aren't concerned about anything but themselves. And I'm always happy to see a relevant ministry.

It's alright to talk about "long white robes over yonder," in all of its symbolism. But ultimately people want some suits and dresses and shoes to wear down here. It's alright to talk about "streets flowing with milk and honey," but God has commanded us to be concerned about the slums down here, and his children who can't eat three square meals a day. It's alright to talk about the new Jerusalem, but one day, God's preacher must talk about the New York, the new Atlanta, the new Philadelphia, the new Los Angeles, the new Memphis, Tennessee. This is what we have to do.

Now the other thing we'll have to do is this: Always anchor our external direct action with the power of economic withdrawal. Now, we are poor people, individually, we are poor when you compare us with white society in America. We are poor. Never stop and forget that collectively, that means all of us together, collectively we are richer than all the nations in the world, with the exception of nine. Did you ever think about that? After you leave the United States, Soviet Russia, Great Britain, West Germany, France, and I could name the others, the Negro collectively is richer than most nations of the world. We have an annual income of more than thirty billion dollars a year, which is more than all of the exports of the United States, and more than the national budget of Canada. Did you know that? That's power right there, if we know how to pool it.

We don't have to argue with anybody. We don't have to curse and go around acting bad with our words. We don't need any bricks and bottles, we don't need any Molotov cocktails, we just need to go around to these stores, and to these massive industries in our country, and say, "God sent us by here, to say to you that you're not treating his children right. And we've come by here to ask you to make the first item on your agenda—fair treatment, where God's children are concerned. Now, if you are not prepared to do that, we do have an agenda that we must follow. And our agenda calls for withdrawing economic support from you."

And so, as a result of this, we are asking you tonight, to go out and tell your neighbors not to buy Coca-Cola in Memphis. Go by and tell them not to buy Sealtest milk. Tell them not to buy—what is the other bread?—Wonder Bread. And what is the other bread company, Jesse? Tell them not to buy Hart's bread. As Jesse Jackson has said, up to now, only the garbage men have been feeling pain; now we must kind of redistribute the pain. We are choosing these companies because they haven't been fair in their hiring policies; and we are choosing them because they can begin the process of saying, they are going to support the needs and the rights of these men who are on strike. And then they can move on downtown and tell Mayor Loeb to do what is right.

But not only that, we've got to strengthen black institutions. I call upon you to take your money out of the banks downtown and deposit your money in Tri-State Bank—we want a "bank-in" movement in Memphis. So go by the savings and loan association. I'm not asking you something that we don't do ourselves at SCLC. Judge Hooks and others will tell you that we have an account here in the savings and loan association from the Southern Christian Leadership Conference. We're just telling you to follow what we're doing. Put your money there. You have six or seven black insurance companies in Memphis. Take out your insurance there. We want to have an "insurance-in."

Now these are some practical things we can do. We begin the process of building a greater economic base. And at the same time, we are putting pressure where it really hurts. I ask you to follow through here.

Now, let me say as I move to my conclusion that we've got to give ourselves to this struggle until the end. Nothing would be more tragic than to stop at this point, in Memphis. We've got to see it through. And when we have our march, you need to be there. Be concerned about your brother. You may not be on strike. But either we go up together, or we go down together.

Let us develop a kind of dangerous unselfishness. One day a man came to Jesus; and he wanted to raise some questions about some vital matters in life. At points, he wanted to trick

Jesus, and show him that he knew a little more than Jesus knew, and through this, throw him off base. Now that question could have easily ended up in a philosophical and theological debate. But Jesus immediately pulled that question from mid-air, and placed it on a dangerous curve between Jerusalem and Jericho. And he talked about a certain man, who fell among thieves. You remember that a Levite and a priest passed by on the other side. They didn't stop to help him. And finally a man of another race came by. He got down from his beast, decided nc _ to be compassionate by proxy. But with him, administered first aid, and helped the man in need. Jesus ended up saying, this was the good man, this was the great man, because he had the capacity to project the "I" into the "thou," and to be concerned about his brother. Now you know, we use our imagination a great deal to try to determine why the priest and the Levite didn't stop. At times we say they were busy going to church meetings—an ecclesiastical gathering—and they had to get on down to Jerusalem so they wouldn't be late for their meeting. At other times we would speculate that there was a religious law that "One who was engaged in religious ceremonials was not to touch a human body twenty-four hours before the ceremony." And every now and then we begin to wonder whether maybe they were not going down to Jerusalem, or down to Jericho, rather to organize a "Jericho Road Improvement Association." That's a possibility. Maybe they felt that it was better to deal with the problem from the casual root, rather than to get bogged down with an individual effort.

But I'm going to tell you what my imagination tells me. It's possible that these men were afraid. You see, the Jericho road is a dangerous road. I remember when Mrs. King and I were first in Jerusalem. We rented a car and drove from Jerusalem down to Jericho. And as soon as we got on that road, I said to my wife, "I can see why Jesus used this as a setting for his parable." It's a winding, meandering road. It's really conducive for ambushing. You start out in Jerusalem, which is about 1200 miles, or rather 1200 feet above sea level. And by the time you get down to Jericho, fifteen or twenty minutes later, you're about 2200 feet below sea level. That's a dangerous road. In the days of Jesus it came to be known as the "Bloody Pass." And you know, it's possible that the priest and the Levite looked over that man on the ground and wondered if the robbers were still around. Or it's possible that they felt that the man on the ground was merely faking. And he was acting like he had been robbed and hurt, in order to seize them over there, lure them for quick and easy seizure. And so the first question that the Levite asked was, "If I stop to help this man, what will happen to me?" But then the Good Samaritan came by. And he reversed the question: "If I do not stop to help this man, what will happen to him?"

That's the question before you tonight. Not, "If I stop to help the sanitation workers, what will happen to all of the hours that I usually spend in my office every day and every week as a pastor?" The question is not, "If I stop to help this man in need, what will happen to me?" "If I do not stop to help the sanitation workers, what will happen to them?" That's the question.

Let us rise up tonight with a greater readiness. Let us stand with a greater determination. And let us move on in these powerful days, these days of challenge to make America what it ought to be. We have an opportunity to make America a better nation. And I want to thank God, once more, for allowing me to be here with you.

You know, several years ago, I was in New York City autographing the first book that I had written. And while sitting there autographing books, a demented black woman came up. The only question I heard from her was, "Are you Martin Luther King?"

And I was looking down writing, and I said yes. And the next minute I felt something beating on my chest. Before I knew it I had been stabbed by this demented woman. I was rushed to Harlem Hospital. It was a dark Saturday afternoon. And that blade had gone through, and the X-rays revealed that the tip of the blade was on the edge of my aorta, the main artery. And once that's punctured, you drown in your own blood—that's the end of you.

It came out in the *New York Times* the next morning, that if I had sneezed, I would have died. Well, about four days later, they allowed me, after the operation, after my chest had been opened, and the blade had been taken out, to move around in the wheel chair in the hospital. They allowed me to read some of the mail that came in, and from all over the states, and the world, kind letters came in. I read a few, but one of them I will never forget. I had received one from the President and the Vice-President. I've forgotten what those telegrams said. I'd received a visit and a letter from the Governor of New York, but

I've forgotten what the letter said. But there was another letter that came from a little girl, a young girl who was a student at the White Plains High School. And I looked at that letter, and I'll never forget it. It said simply, "Dear Dr. King: I am a ninth-grade student at the White Plains High School." She said, "While it should not matter, I would like to mention that I am a white girl. I read in the paper of your misfortune, and of your suffering. And I read that if you had sneezed, you would have died. And I'm simply writing you to say that I'm so happy that you didn't sneeze."

And I want to say tonight, I want to say that I am happy that I didn't sneeze. Because if I had sneezed, I wouldn't have been around here in 1960, when students all over the South started sitting-in at lunch counters. And I knew that as they were sitting in, they were really standing up for the best in the American dream. And taking the whole nation back to those great walls of democracy which were dug deep by the Founding Fathers in the Declaration of Independence and the Constitution. If I had sneezed, I wouldn't have been around in 1962, when Negroes in Albany, Georgia, decided to straighten their backs up. And whenever men and women straighten their backs up, they are going somewhere, because a man can't ride your back unless it is bent. If I had sneezed, I wouldn't have been here in 1963, when the black people of Birmingham, Alabama, aroused the conscience of this nation, and brought into being the Civil Rights Bill. If I had sneezed, I wouldn't have had a chance later that year, in August, to try to tell America about a dream that I had had. If I had sneezed, I wouldn't have been down in Selma, Alabama, to see the great movement there. If I had sneezed, I wouldn't have been in Memphis to see a community rally around those brothers and sisters who are suffering. I'm so happy that I didn't sneeze.

And they were telling me, now it doesn't matter now. It really doesn't matter what happens now. I left Atlanta this morning, and as we got started on the plane, there were six of us, the pilot said over the public address system, "We are sorry for the delay, but we have Dr. Martin Luther King on the plane. And to be sure that all of the bags were checked, and to be sure that nothing would be wrong with the plane, we had to check out everything carefully. And we've had the plane protected and guarded all night."

And then I got into Memphis. And some began to say the threats, or talk about the threats that were out. What would happen to me from some of our sick white brothers?

Well, I don't know what will happen now. We've got some difficult days ahead. But it doesn't matter with me now. Because I've been to the mountaintop. And I don't mind. Like anybody, I would like to live a long life. Longevity has its place. But I'm not concerned about that now. I just want to do God's will. And He's allowed me to go up to the mountain. And I've looked over. And I've seen the promised land. I may not get there with you. But I want you to know tonight, that we, as a people will get to the promised land. And I'm happy, tonight. I'm not worried about anything. I'm not fearing any man. Mine eyes have seen the glory of the coming of the Lord.

Eagle Rock

Alice Walker

In the town where I was born
There is a mound
Some eight feet high
That from the ground
Seems piled up stones
In Georgia
Insignificant.

But from above
The lookout tower
Floor
An eagle widespread
In solid gravel
Stone
Takes shape
Below;

The Cherokees raised it
Long ago
Before westward journeys
In the snow
Before the
National Policy slew
Long before Columbus knew.

I used to stop and
Linger there
Within the cleanswept tower stair
Rock Eagle pinesounds
Rush of stillness
Lifting up my hair.

Pinned to the earth
The eagle endures
The Cherokees are gone
The people come on tours.
And on surrounding National
Forest lakes the air rings
With cries
The silenced make.

Wearing cameras
They never hear
But relive their victory
Every year
And take it home
With them.
Young Future Farmers
As paleface warriors
Grub
Live off the land

Pretend Indian, therefore
Man,
Can envision a lake
But never a flood
On earth
So cleanly scrubbed
Of blood:
They come before the rock
Jolly conquerors.

They do not know the rock
They love
Lives and is bound
To bide its time
To wrap its stony wings
Around
The innocent eager 4-H Club.

Cat-Like

John Holman

MY brother and his wife got a white persian cat from some-place, a richer friend I guess. They brought it around my par-ents' house when it was a kitten, a white fluff bounding about my cuffs. Its name was Omar. I was fourteen. Omar grew to be fluffier, delicate and more beautiful, and turned out to be a girl. She got pregnant as soon as she was of age, and had trouble de-livering her litter. She had made a nest under a bush in front of the house. My brother, his wife, and I stood around wondering how to help her until Omar in anguish got up from her kittens and started walking around with the job visibly half done, a kit-ten dangling. Squeamish about the whole birth process, and sick about poor Omar and the sight of her distress, I told them to do something, anything, call a vet why don't you. They had no money, that's why they didn't.

My brother, accepting his responsibility as owner of the cat, caught up with Omar around the corner of the house and gave her the necessary assistance. That kitten was stillborn, but the others survived. Omar, beautiful, proud and exotic, was to me a symbol of their young marriage. It was a marriage of college teenagers with bright expectations, and Omar was as grand as their promise. She represented what I thought was our foreign essence and our exquisite potential. Omar was not supposed to be an outdoor cat, but because we were outdoor boys and my brother's city-bred wife was adventuresome herself, Omar lived her version of our lives—she did what the other cats did; she fought, climbed trees and caught birds. And she liked it. But she was born for something else, and she looked as though she knew it. I don't remember what finally happened to her. My brother and his wife eventually divorced. Maybe Omar was put up for adoption.

Cat-wise, I was not unprepared when the woman I was pur-suing finally let me in her house and introduced me to her cat. She lived in Raleigh and I lived in Durham, and I had met her while we taught at St. Augustine's College. No question, she was the glowingest presence on campus, in town. She had a boyfriend but finally got tired of him. He wasn't easy to shake. I got in on a night when he threatened to come over despite her asking him not to. She was afraid, she said to me when I phoned her. He wasn't acting right. I'll tell you what, I said, why don't I be there when he comes. O.K., she said. But, he's a Vietnam vet.

I'd seen him, of course. He was tall, big. Still, I showered and drove to Raleigh. Chances were that he wouldn't make a fuss. Being a trained killer, he was probably choosy about whom he beat up. Besides, he already was looking nearly foolish and I was betting he wouldn't risk being an all-out creep. He had a high-priced sports car and he cared what people thought about him, what he thought of himself, which was why he was being so stubborn in the first place.

I pulled slowly into the parking lot of the apartment complex, scanning for his car. At her door, I thought that he might already be inside, forgetting already that I hadn't seen his car, then remembering, then thinking that he might be skilled in concealment. But it was my own obsession's glowing face before me when the door opened. *She* didn't look worried. She looked happy to see me. She led me inside her small apartment and we sat to wait for the soldier to show up. We listened to her jazz records and drank her beer.

She had antique furniture from a flea market, a good deal, she told me. The chair I sat in was big and green, and when I looked closely I could make out how pretty the fabric must have been before it faded; there were tiny gold flowers threaded into the small triangle patterns, with pink centers. I tried to be calm in that chair while in the kitchen she stirred a pot of spaghetti sauce—my last meal, I told myself, if it got served soon.

About then her cat jumped from nowhere onto my lap. I didn't know she had a cat, hadn't seen it, heard it, or smelled it, but I accepted it as calmly as I did the yellow flowers in the fabric of the chair. It was a tabby-point, my hostess explai   ' to me later, part siamese and part tabby; it looked part   .ey, its tail and legs subtly grey-striped and its body pale sand. Its eyes were blue and its face was faintly striped beneath the soft-grey ears. While the jazz piano trickled from the stereo speakers, I scratched the cat's head, and when I stopped it nudged my hand for more.

I was in that way occupied when Carmen came from the kitchen with a fresh bottle of beer for me. I was told that I was cuddling Kitty Kat, whom she had found lost and mewing in a littered supermarket parking lot, a kitten filthy with motor oil and dirt. She had brought it home, cleaned it up. While I listened to her story, Kitty Kat purred deeply and pranced, sinking its claws into the cloth of my corduroys—a new pair to look my best—and I was trying to shift and shrink in my clothes to avoid the sharp claw points. It was in my favor that Kitty Kat liked me enough to stay in the chair with me.

I sat like that at least an hour—the cat going to sleep, Carmen changing records—forgetting the menace of the angry boyfriend who never arrived. We talked, finally ate, and I went home, only to visit again and again until two years later we married. With the marriage, the Kitty Kat became mine. She would be inches from my face when I woke up in the mornings. My wife's face and my cat's face were similarly shaped—oval—and they both had cool bright eyes with aspects mysterious lazing and lurking deep behind them. My wife's eyes are light brown, like stream pebbles, and I thought of her as a forest creature. I began to suspect that she was a cat reincarnated as human, that she might have formerly possessed feline eyes that watched glowing from behind forest leaves.

Kitty Kat lived eighteen very dignified years. She moved from Raleigh to Greensboro, to Durham, to Winston-Salem, to Hattiesburg, back to Winston-Salem, to Tampa. She visited Atlanta often. She walked across the pages of books I tried to read. She brushed against my hand as I tried to write, wanting a scratch. She woke me up early mornings when I thought no one but I knew of my plan to wake and work before dawn. She roused me when a pipe burst under the kitchen sink. She brought birds in the house. She caught a bat and struggled with it on our bed in the middle of the night, terrifying us. (A struggle of consonants, still a terror.) She played with chipmunks until they died, tore their hearts out. She ignored the roaches in Mississippi, to our disappointment, but was fond of lizards. One midnight in Mississippi, she hooked a claw in the flesh of my little finger when I fetched her from the roof of a car stereo shop. For several puzzling minutes, we were joined. The wound healed in a day.

When she died, our hearts broke, and we got another cat, rescuing it from a flea-infested house of dogs, a cat that looked like Kitty Kat. Sarafina had one litter when she was seven months old. I feared she would have difficulty, like Omar, but we were fortunate to know some veterinary students whom it was my wife's job to advise. A good student came over, stood vigil. When my children left for school in the morning we had four kittens, and when they came home we had seven. It was my daughter's birthday, too—she was nine years old. *Her* birth had been frightening, difficult and dangerous, just as I had suspected, but we had a good doctor that day, also.

We kept one kitten, a solid grey boy with a wide face. It looked like a tiny bear, so our son named it Bear Cat. Sarafina was killed by a car two weeks before we moved from Tampa. But by then Bear Cat was grown. Once he brought home a bird, let it go in the house, and while it flew through the room he leapt off the arm of a chair and caught it. Most impressive.

I've written a story that has a cat in it, a dirty alley cat with white dry wounds on its haunches and head. That cat might be for all the cats in my life. It is a grand, wounded, striving, lucky animal, an obnoxious object of great generosity. I suspect now that it was the dignifying influence of Carmen's Kitty Kat that caused her angry boyfriend to rethink his threat those years ago. Certainly Omar, Kitty Kat, Sarafina and Bear Cat have forced me to confront their awesome respectability. These cats amaze me. They are beautiful show-offs. They eat other animals raw. They carry their suffering with dignity. They get what they want. They let you love them. Perhaps all my two-legged characters are, as with my fantasy about my wife, cats reincarnated, creatures admirable and disturbing that I'll never understand.

Biographical Notes

Thomas Jefferson (1743–1826)   Though best remembered for drafting the Declaration of Independence, the third United States president wrote eloquently on a wide range of topics, including his native state. *Notes on Virginia,* published in 1784, was Jefferson's response to a series of questions posed by the secretary of the French Legation at Philadelphia.

Henry Timrod (1828–1867) Ironically, the war that devastated this poet's homeland was the inspiration for his best poetry. A native of Charleston, South Carolina, Timrod served briefly in the Confederate Army, then worked as a war correspondent, writing his most important poems during or immediately after the Civil War. Because of his patriotic themes and dedication to the Confederate cause, Timrod has been called the "Laureate of the Confederacy."

Sidney Lanier (1842–1881) The musical quality of his poetry attests to the fact that aside from being a gifted poet, Sidney Lanier was also a talented musician. Born in Macon, Georgia, Lanier believed that poetry should have the natural rhythm and fluidity of music and that the sound of a poem should reinforce its meaning.

Booker T. Washington (1856–1915) The founder and first president of Alabama's Tuskegee Institute, Booker T. Washington was the most prominent African American of the late nineteenth century. In 1901, Washington published his best-selling autobiography, *Up from Slavery,* from which "The Struggle for an Education" is excerpted.

John Crowe Ransom (1888–1974) As a young man, this Tennesseean native was one of the Fugitives, a group of poets that also included Robert Penn Warren and Allen Tate. Over time Ransom developed a unique style in which he contrasted the deep feelings expressed in his poems with a sense of detachment from those feelings. Ransom is also noted for establishing the *Kenyon Review,* one of the most important literary journals of our time.

Thomas Wolfe (1900–1938) A man of tremendous energy, emotion, and height (he stood six feet six inches tall), Thomas

Wolfe grew up in a large, eccentric family in Asheville, North Carolina. In his writing, which includes five novels and many short stories and works of nonfiction, Wolfe often drew on his personal experiences. Although his career was brief, Wolfe's use of vivid imagery and lyrical language helped establish him as an important twentieth century writer.

Margaret Mitchell (1900–1949) After resigning from her job as a newspaper reporter in Atlanta, Georgia, Margaret Mitchell began to write a story of the Civil War and Reconstruction that was set in her home state. Published in 1935, *Gone With the Wind* sold one million copies in its first six months, won the Pulitzer Prize for Literature, and was made into a movie that received ten Academy Awards. Despite—or perhaps because of—the success of her first effort, Mitchell never published again.

William Faulkner (1897–1962) One of the most prominent figures in American literature, William Faulkner grew up in Oxford, Mississippi. Although he never finished high school, Faulkner was a voracious reader who developed an early interest in writing. In his highly innovative novels and short stories, Faulkner experimented with narrative chronology, explored multiple points of view, and delved deeply into the minds of his characters. In 1950 he was awarded the Nobel Prize for Literature.

Carson McCullers (1917–1967) In her writing, Carson McCullers poignantly captured the feelings of isolation and loneliness sometimes experienced by people living in a large and seemingly indifferent world. Born in Columbus, Georgia, McCullers displayed a great deal of musical talent as a young girl. When she was seventeen she traveled to New York City to pursue a musical career, but took up writing instead. She published "Wunderkind," her first story, when she was only nineteen.

James Still (born 1906) A descendant of pioneers who settled in the Appalachian Mountains, James Still grew up in northern Alabama and later moved to Kentucky. Along with Jesse Stuart, Still has long been considered one of the country's leading Appalachian writers. Like his first novel, *River of Earth,* all of Still's books and poems chronicle life in this mountain region of the United States.

Eudora Welty (born 1909) This Pulitzer Prize winner, who has spent most of her life in Jackson, Mississippi, is one of the South's most highly regarded writers. Her short stories and novels, set in the deep south, feature a strong sense of place and distinctive narrative voices. "A Visit of Charity" originally appeared in *A Curtain of Green*, Welty's first short story collection, which was published in 1941.

Margaret Walker (born 1915) A leading voice in African American literature, Margaret Walker has called her poems "the songs of my people." Walker was born and grew up in Birmingham, Alabama, where her father was a Methodist minister. She taught for many years at Jackson State College in Mississippi, where she also directed an institute for the advancement of African American life and culture.

Jesse Stuart (1907–1984) In his novels, poems, and short stories, Jesse Stuart has depicted with humor and sympathy the mountain people of his home state of Kentucky. Born in a one-room log cabin in W-Hollow, Greenup County, Stuart spent most of his life as a writer and teacher. One of Kentucky's most prominent literary voices, in 1954 Stuart was made poet laureate of his native state.

Flannery O'Connor (1925–1964) Although her life and career were brief, this native of Savannah, Georgia, remains an American writer of great prominence. Her two novels and two volumes of short stories contain her trademark techniques: sudden acts of violence, grotesque humor, and characters who are misfits or social outcasts. Through her exaggerated, often shocking tales, O'Connor has forced readers to confront such human faults as hypocrisy, insensitivity, self-centeredness, and prejudice.

James Dickey (born 1923) A lover of nature and a devoted outdoorsman, James Dickey has been a high school football player, a fighter pilot in World War II and the Korean War, and a highly respected poet and writer. A native of Atlanta, Georgia, Dickey has received acclaim for his poetry as well as for his successful novel, *Deliverance*. That novel inspired a motion picture in which Dickey appeared in the role of a sheriff.

Wendell Berry (born 1934) A writer and farmer, this Kentucky native's poems, essays, and fiction reflect his love and abiding respect for the land. After spending time as a young man in California, Europe, and New Y' 'k City, Berry returned to the Kentucky land that was settled by his family in the late 1800's. He taught for many years at the University of Kentucky before resigning to devote all of his time to farming and writing.

Martin Luther King, Jr. (1929–1968) One of the most dynamic civil rights leaders of the twentieth century, Dr. Martin Luther King, Jr., galvanized supporters with his impassioned speeches and well-publicized demonstrations. Born in Atlanta, Georgia, King went on to serve as a Baptist minister in Montgomery, Alabama. He delivered his speech, "I've Been to the Mountaintop," just one day before his assassination in 1968.

Alice Walker (born 1944) As the youngest of eight children, Alice Walker says she spent a good deal of her childhood seeking out peace and quiet. Growing up in Eatonton, Georgia, Walker began keeping a journal and writing poems when she was eight years old. During her career she has published poetry, short stories, novels, and nonfiction. Her novel *The Color Purple* won the Pulitzer Prize for Literature and was made into an acclaimed motion picture.

John Holman (born 1951) This writer, who was born in Durham, North Carolina, has taught English in universities in his native state, in Mississippi, and in his current home state of Florida. His articles, stories, and poems have been published in books and in periodicals, such as *The New Yorker.*

Acknowledgments *(continued from p. ii)*

Alfred A. Knopf, Inc.
"Janet Waking" by John Crowe Ransom, from *Selected Poems.* Copyright 1927 by Alfred A. Knopf, Inc., and renewed 1955 by John Crowe Ransom. Reprinted by permission of the publisher.

William Morris Agency, Inc.
From *Gone With the Wind* by Margaret Mitchell. Copyright © 1936 by Margaret Mitchell. Reprinted by permission of the William Morris Agency, Inc., on behalf of the author's estate.

North Point Press, a division of Farrar, Straus, & Giroux
"That Distant Land" from *The Wild Birds* by Wendell Berry. Copyright © 1985, 1986 by Wendell Berry. Reprinted by permission of North Point Press, a division of Farrar, Straus, & Giroux, Inc.

Princeton University Press
From "Notes on Virginia" by Thomas Jefferson, from *The Papers of Thomas Jefferson,* edited by Julian P. Boyd et al., Vol. I, copyright 1950 by Princeton University Press; Vol. XII, copyright © 1955 by Princeton University Press.

Random House, Inc.
"A Rose for Emily" from *Collected Stories of William Faulkner* by William Faulkner. Copyright 1930 and renewed 1958 by William Faulkner. "Spotted Horses" from *Uncollected Stories of William Faulkner* by William Faulkner, edited by Joseph Blotner. Copyright 1931 and renewed 1959 by William Faulkner. Copyright 1940 and renewed 1968 by Estelle Faulkner and Jill Faulkner Summers. Reprinted by permission of Random House, Inc.

Scribner, a division of Simon & Schuster
"Song of the Chattahoochee" and "The Marshes of Glynn" from *Poems of Sidney Lanier,* edited by his Wife. Copyright 1884, 1891 by Mary Lanier. Published by Charles Scribner's Sons. "Circus at Dawn" from *From Death to Morning* by Thomas Wolfe. Copyright 1935 by Charles Scribner's Sons, renewal copyright © 1963 Paul Gitlin. Reprinted with the permission of Scribner, a division of Simon & Schuster.

James Still
River of Earth by James Still. Copyright 1940 by James Still. Copyright © 1978 by The University Press of Kentucky. Reprinted by permission of the author.

Jesse Stuart Foundation
"Another April" from *Tales From the Plum Grove Hills* by Jesse Stuart. Copyright © 1942, 1946 Jesse Stuart. © renewed Jesse Stuart and Jesse Stuart Foundation. Reprinted by permission of Jesse Stuart Foundation, P.O. Box #391, Ashland, KY 41114.

Wesleyan University Press
"Sled Burial Dream Ceremony" by James Dickey, from *James Dickey: Poems 1957–1967.* Copyright © 1958, 1959, 1960, 1961, 1962, 1963, 1964, 1965, 1966, 1967 by James Dickey.

The Wylie Agency
"Cat-Like" by John Holman. Copyright © 1996 by John Holman. First published in *In Short: A Collection of Brief Creative Nonfiction,* edited by Judith Kitchen and Mary Paumier Jones. Reprinted with permission of The Wylie Agency, Inc.

Note: Every effort has been made to locate the copyright owner of material reprinted in this book. Omissions brought to our attention will be corrected in subsequent editions.